Gathering Together Volume 1: Christian Fellowship

Gathering Together Volume 1: Christian Fellowship

Lance Lambert

LANCE LAMBERT MINISTRIES

Richmond, Virginia, USA

978-1-68389-018-8
www.lancelambert.org

Contents

Introduction _____ 7

1. Why We Meet Together _____ 9

2. The Headship of Christ _____ 41

3. The Heavenly Church_____ 73

4. Organism Versus Organisation _____ 107

5. The Church — The Fellowship of Christ _____ 137

6. The Oneness of Christ _____ 171

Introduction

What is the church?
What is the basis for meeting together as the church?
What is true fellowship?
What is the priesthood of all believers?
What is the difference between unity
and uniformity in the church?

In this book, the first volume of *Gathering Together*, Lance Lambert answers these questions and many more. In doing this, he emphasizes the absolute headship of Christ and the oneness of the body of Christ.

The content of these pages is the transcription of six messages given in 1968 by Lance Lambert. He gave this series of messages to Christians meeting together at Halford House, Richmond, Surrey, England. The complete series contained twelve messages under the title *Meeting Together*. This book is published as Volume One, "The Church—The Fellowship of Christ." It maintains Lance's spoken style, in his classic British English, with minimal editing for clarity.

Nearly fifty years have passed since these words were spoken, but the need for them remains great, as the coming of the Lord Jesus draws near. May God bless His people and use this book to the fulfillment of His purpose.

1.
Why We Meet Together

1 Corinthians 1:1–9

Paul, called to be an apostle of Jesus Christ through the will of God, and Sosthenes our brother, unto the church of God which is at Corinth, even them that are sanctified in Christ Jesus, called [to be] saints, with all that call upon the name of our Lord Jesus Christ in every place, their Lord and ours: Grace to you and peace from God our Father and the Lord Jesus Christ. I thank my God always concerning you, for the grace of God which was given you in Christ Jesus; that in everything ye were enriched in him, in all utterance and all knowledge; even as the testimony of Christ was confirmed in you: so that ye come behind in no gift; waiting for the revelation of our Lord Jesus Christ; who shall also confirm you unto the end, that ye be unreprovable in the day of our Lord Jesus Christ. God is faithful, through whom ye were called into the fellowship of his Son Jesus Christ our Lord. [What a word for the church at Corinth, of all places!]

Now I beseech you, brethren, through the name of our Lord Jesus Christ, that ye all speak the same thing, and that there be no divisions among you; but that ye be perfected together in the same mind and in the same judgment. For it hath been signified unto me concerning you, my brethren, by them that are of the household of Chloe, that there are contentions among you. Now this I mean, that each one of you saith, I am of Paul; and I am of Apollos; and I am of Cephas; and I of Christ. Is Christ divided? was Paul crucified for you? or were ye baptized into the name of Paul?

At a study session with the brothers and sisters at Halford House, Lance presented the question, "Why are you here at Halford House?" The replies were as follows:

"God wanted me here."

"I found the Lord here."

"The Lord brought me here. I found there to be more truth here according to the gospel in the New Testament rather than what I see in the world today."

"He saved me here."

"I saw more truth."

"I found a place to meet with God's people, to grow spiritually and so that I can help others."

"I found life here."

"There is more prayer, supplication here."

"Because I belong to Christ and not to a church."

"I am learning about myself."

"The Lord wants to do something corporately, together with others."

"It is home here."

Why are we here? I think we can sum up these answers, most of which are false, (but we are all in the boat together) as friendliness and fellowship. Under that title will come quite a number of the answers we had. You are coming here because you find a friendliness and spiritual fellowship, and therefore you prefer to come here than go, perhaps, to an Anglican Church up the hill or a Brethren Assembly across the river or a Free Church in the centre of the town because you get more fellowship here than there. That is one thing.

Another reason for coming, which I did not hear from anyone, but we will put down lest there are some who may feel it, is the freedom of the Spirit. Some people say, "I come to Halford House because it is less organised. I do not like the organised type of church; it is too liturgical. (Someone has said, 'suffocating.') I feel there is a freedom here." Of course, we have a long way to go, but there is a freedom of the Spirit here.

A third one I think we can put down is the measure of Christ. Now this is a very spiritual reason. This includes two things—the amount of spiritual life and spiritual food. In other words, you come here because you find more of Christ here than anywhere else. That is how you feel; it is a subjective thing. Someone else might not feel it. But you feel that here in this company there is more of Christ, more spiritual life, and more spiritual food; therefore you come here. That is the basis of your gathering. If you find another company with more of the Lord than at

Halford House you leave. If you can find more spiritual food or more spiritual life elsewhere, you are going where you find something more. That is another reason.

The fourth reason is because you were saved here. That is quite a good reason. You were saved here, therefore you do not know anywhere else. You feel it is your home.

The last reason is the will of God.

Those five reasons cover all but two of the answers we have had. In other words, two of the answers were correct. These five cover the general reasons why people are either in this place or that place. If you think about it, with any of these reasons you could be in a Baptist Church, a Congregational Church, a Brethren Assembly, the Salvation Army, the Quakers, the Pentecostals, the peculiar people, sometimes called the Protestant Peculiars or the Strict Baptists or the General or the State Church, or anywhere else. The point is you will go where you can get fellowship. So if there is more fellowship in St. Mary's rather than the Gospel Hall down by the railway sidings, you are going to go to St. Mary's because there is more fellowship there, more friendliness there. There is a pleasant circle of people there, and they are all very cosy and friendly and warm and you get a certain amount of fellowship there. You could take all of these.

The Will of God

Now, obviously, the will of God is one that we have to be careful with, yet, we can use this matter of the will of God in a very subjective way, in an altogether wrong way. In other words, our deceitful hearts can say to us something like this: "I am here because it is the will of God," but when I fall out with brother so and so it is no longer the will of God. Suddenly I cannot stay here any longer. There is a collision with someone, and then immediately you discover it is the will of God to move on somewhere else. In other words, you have a fire escape. When things get too hot, you can use the fire escape and leave, and the fire escape is the will of God. Now, I am not saying that this is the will of God; that is precisely what it is not; but we all gloss things over with the term, "the will of God."

So that is why I say in actual fact, if we understand what the will of the Lord is, really understand what the will of the Lord is, as it says in Ephesians 5:17, we are trapped. We are absolutely trapped. But we can use this matter of the will of God in a falsely subjective way, not knowing our deceitful hearts, in order to be able to get out of certain circumstances, of difficult brothers and sisters or others that we just cannot get on with; we would rather run away from them.

The Basis for Our Fellowship

Now, I am saying all these points are important for us to understand, but not one of them preserves the unity of Christ. Not one of them. Not even the measure of Christ preserves the unity of Christ. Why? Of course, if you think of it theoretically it should. For where there is more of the Lord, there should be the greater appreciation for the oneness of Christ; but is that always the case? Often when there is a measure of the Lord, we can become very superior and think that we are the elite, and our very understanding of the measure of the Lord makes us divisive.

So this is the whole point. The ground of the church, the basis for our fellowship together is the preservation of the unity of Christ, the preservation of the unity of the Spirit. Therefore we have got to discover what the basis of our fellowship is. All these things may be right as additional things, but they are not sufficient for a basis of gathering together. Will they keep us together? Within ten years, we might all have said farewell to one another on these points, certainly on the first three and the last one. So I hope I make it clear. First of all, we made our mistakes and now we are a little nearer to an understanding or at least a little more alive if we ask ourselves: Why are we here at Halford House?

Why Do We Gather as We Do?

What are we? Why do we gather together in the manner in which we do here in this company? Are we absolutely clear as to what the objective of God is and what the basis is upon which God commits Himself? It troubles me greatly when I hear people speaking about coming into the house of the Lord, or speaking of these premises as the house of God. It is quite wrong. This house may be a sign, the bricks and mortar may be a sign, but it is not the house of God. It never was and never will be. However precious the sign and what it signifies, the bricks and mortar are not the house of God.

It also troubles me very greatly when I hear people speaking of this as *the* fellowship. Of course, I do realise that it is rather hard to sort of fumble around and find some word by which we can describe the company that we are in. But "the fellowship" is unfortunate because it is quite unbiblical. The word *fellowship* is never used in the New Testament as *"the"* fellowship ever. That is why for those of you who perhaps are puzzled over it and for those of you who have never even noticed it, we do not have the definite article before the word "Christian Fellowship". We do not call it "The Christian Fellowship." You will see on the headed paper or on the stone outside "Christian Fellowship." It is not a title; it is a description. So, it is not "The Fellowship," and may we all be delivered from referring to it as such. It is better, I think, if you want to use a good Biblical word to call it "the company." Remember Peter and John, when they were released, went to their own company in Jerusalem.

It is because of this confusion there is amongst us, that we have felt led by the Lord to embark once more upon this matter. We took it up some years ago beginning in 1957. Now again we want to look at the matter and trust that the Lord will use these times to get us clear, old and young, as to what the Lord's objective is and what that basis is to which He will commit Himself in these days.

What is the Lord Seeking to Do?

Why has the Lord so remarkably and amazingly led us and provided for us, setting His seal upon our history in so many ways? It is not that we are anything in ourselves. We never tire of saying, "We must be the biggest collection of dumb clucks in the world, *saved* dumb clucks. Nevertheless, we are but a collection of fools, and the Lord has done something for us." However, we have to say that we have an amazing story of the Lord's faithfullness, and provision, and leadership in minute ways as well as large ways. Why has the Lord so singularly committed Himself?

What lies at the root of it? Should we not ask ourselves what it is the Lord is seeking to do and why?

Are we just another non-denominational, evangelical church of which there are quite a number? Are we a kind of non-denominational, evangelical church with a minister who wears normal clothes and is called Mr., and where the assistant minister has a full time job at University Corinth? Is that the kind of group we are, just an evangelical church like that? Or are we a fellowship more informal, less organized which is catering to the needs of lonely people in a highly-urbanized society? They do not get what they need in the normal evangelical church (friendliness and fellowship), so they are drawn irresistibly in this highly-urbanized society. Is that what we are here for to provide them with a cup of tea and some fellowship in a nice "homey" surrounding?

Now do not get me wrong. There is such a thing as fellowship. Fellowship is the hallmark of the true church, and love is the power of the true church. The fact of feeling at home can be an altogether spiritual matter; because if God is at home, you are at home. So let us not despise the person who says, "I feel at home here; this is my home." That is right, providing it is because God is at home, we are at home. It is God's dwelling place. It is not in the bricks and mortar, not in the place, but in the company.

What Are We?

What are we? Are we a kind of evangelistic mission seeking to reach needy men and women with an emphasis on juvenile delinquents? Is that what we are, in a matter that God has singularly blessed us? Or are we a group of Christians, a company of Christians emphasizing some particular aspect of truth or some particular experience of the cross or Spirit that we feel to be vital? Is that what we are? Or are we a group of Christians who feel called together to support and uphold a particularly anointed minister (if you should feel that way about me)? Is that what we are? So then we become a people centred in a ministry, and therefore because the ministry is entrusted to one person, it is centred in that one person. Is that what we are? Is that what we are called to? Is that what God is seeking to do with us and amongst us? What are we? Good question.

Why Meet Separately from Other Groups?

Let us imagine that a leading evangelical minister or leader has approached us and is asking us a question. His question is this: Why do you meet separately at Halford House? Why do you not join one of the sound and keen denominational churches which are found in your area? Or if you do not like denominationalism, why do you not join one of the ones that is interdenominational in character and outlook? Why do you have to be a separate entity? Why do you not throw in your lot with some other cause of God which is nearer to your way of thinking? Or if you do not like interdenominationalism, you feel that is a halfway house, why not throw in your lot with a nondenominational place? There is one just across your garden, been there since 1736, the oldest free church in Richmond. Why do you not throw in your lot with them? (Not that we would all be able to get in there.) This is the question we are to imagine that we have been asked.

Now, our leading evangelical minister friend says to us: "If you do not like organisation, why don't you join with the Quakers? Why do you start some new group? Or why don't you go to the Open Brethren and join them? Aren't they the same as you? They have no membership." Are we an Open Brethren Assembly who allows sisters to take part? What are we?

Now our dear learned friend continues to ask a few more searching questions. He says, "You are, whether you like it or not, an evangelical company. You may not like the name but you are an evangelical church. Why don't you join the Richmond District Evangelistic Counsel? Why do you stand apart? Furthermore, why do you not join the World Evangelical Alliance, for the whole of the gambit is there from Quakers up to High Church people? Surely you could find your place amongst them. You have only got to accept certain fundamental doctrines which you do. Why don't you belong to the World Evangelical Alliance along with Dr. Lloyd Jones, who also does not belong to it. How is it that you are outside of the World Evangelical Alliance? I understand you do not like the World Evangelical Alliance, but what about the Fellowship of Independent Evangelical Churches? Is that not up your street? Is that not your cup of tea? Aren't you an Independent Evangelical Church? Why don't you come into the FIEC?" Do you know how you would answer these questions? How would you answer this brother if he asked you?

You must understand that none of these answers hold water. He is not going to be impressed by you saying, "There is fellowship there." He is going to say, "That is not the point. You go and put some fellowship in the other place. You are just a selfish person. 'Me, me, me; I go there because I get fellowship. I go there because it is friendly. I go there because I get spiritual food.' You ought to get up from your seat and do something for others for a while and provide a bit of spiritual food for some others." He might say, "You were saved there, yes, that is good; the Lord overrules these mistakes. You got saved there, but your place is to go into these other groups and help them."

Now here is the question, and we need to be able to answer it clearly. What is the justification for our meeting together separately? What is the basis of our gathering? Why are we here at Halford House? As we have said, because of reasons such as friendliness and the fellowship, the measure of Christ, the amount of spiritual life and food, because of a freedom of the spirit, because I was saved there, because I believe it is the will of God that I should be there. Those answers may be good up to a point, but they do not bear the searching scrutiny of the Spirit of God.

The Problem We Face Today

What is the problem? Before we can answer the question: "Why am I at Halford House?" we have to look at the problem. What is the problem that we are confronted with? Let's try and put it as simply as we can. In the New Testament days there was not the complex and intricate problem, which we face as children of God today in the twentieth century. Through the preaching of the gospel many people were saved all over Judea, Samaria and then throughout the whole Roman Empire. As people got saved, as they were born of the Spirit of God, they were simply gathered together in each locality where they lived as the family of God. You were either in the family by spiritual birth or you were not in it. It was as simple as that. Every single believer in any locality belonged to the family. It might only be two, but they were the family there. They represented the family of God in that place. There might have been only two Christians to begin with in Antioch but they were the family of God in Antioch. Your family may be large or may be small, but that is not the point; it is a family. There may be only two of your family in Birmingham and twenty of them in Exeter, but because there are only two in Birmingham, it does not mean they are any less your family. They are your family. They are the only members of your family in Birmingham; there happens to be only two of them. In Exeter there are twenty of them, but it is still your family, no less, no more. They are your kith and kin.

One Church in Each Locality in the First Century

In the first century, there was not the problem we face in the twentieth century. Wherever the gospel went men and women were saved through the power of the Holy Spirit and the preaching of the Word of God. Men and women were gathered together simply as children of God. They were called the *ecclesia*, "the called out ones," the church of God, Jew or Gentile, it made no difference. When they became children of God, whether Jew or Gentile, they were now Christians. They were not Jewish Christians and Gentile Christians; they were Christians. There was no more Jew and no more Gentile, only Christians. It was as simple as that.

I do not know if I have made it as clear as I would like to, but it did not matter where you went, the family of God in each place consisted of those who were born of the Spirit of God and excluded everyone else who was not.

Let me say this again too. In the New Testament there were never two churches in one locality. Never! Hence, they did not face the problem we face today. There was only one church in each locality. The church in Jerusalem, though it numbered at one point at least five thousand people, was never called the churches in Jerusalem, even though they gathered from home to home to break bread. They could not break bread together, so they split them all up in the city in homes and there they broke bread together. It was still the church in Jerusalem. It never became the churches in Jerusalem, not even at the end.

Let me just show you that from the Word of God. Look at Acts 2:41–42: "They then that received his word were baptized: and there were added unto them in that day about three thousand souls. And they continued stedfastly in the apostles' teaching and fellowship, in the breaking of bread and the prayers."

There was no place in Jerusalem which could take three thousand people. So in verse 46 it says, "And day by day, continuing stedfastly with one accord in the temple." They met, all of them together in the temple forecourt. That was the only place they could get the whole lot together for the reading of the word and for prayers. "And breaking bread from home to home, they took their food with gladness and singleness of heart." For the Lord's table they broke up into groups.

In Acts 6:1a, 7 it says, "Now in these days, when the number of the disciples was multiplying...And the word of God increased; and the number of the disciples multiplied in Jerusalem exceedingly; and a great company of the priests were obedient to the faith."

Chapter 8:1: "And there arose on that day a great persecution against the church which was in Jerusalem." Although it numbered many thousands it was still called *the* church that was in Jerusalem and all the way through the New Testament it was always referred to as *the* church in Jerusalem.

In chapter 4:23 there is a very interesting sidelight. "And being let go," (that is Peter and John) "they came to their own company, and reported all that the chief priests and the elders had said unto them." It is a very interesting thing "their own company" because it reveals that the church in Jerusalem had been broken up into smaller groups. Even Peter and John as apostles had their own company. So when they were released, they went directly to their own company and reported to them. Probably they were at prayer. That shows to us that the church at Jerusalem was never divided into churches. There were never two churches in one locality.

The Principle is the Same

Of course, this will immediately raise problems in people's minds. What are you going to do with a city like London? What are you going to do with a city like New York, or Tokyo, or Los Angeles where you have something like ten or eleven million people? That was not a New Testament problem. I quite agree with you that it is a problem, and I do not think we can be legalistic in our approach to this and just say that there must be one church for eleven million people. We have to understand that the Holy Spirit is able to apply and interpret principles for the twentieth century, but the principle remains: one church, one place. You cannot get away from that simple all-important principle.

Then again, I want you to notice this. The church at Corinth might be spiritually poor. It might be rent with factions. It might be carnal in its ways and in its character, but it was still the church at Corinth. Never anywhere is it called anything else but *the* church at Corinth. They were even called "sanctified in Christ Jesus." Any people who were expressing less sanctification, I cannot imagine.

What can we say about the measure of Christ there in the church at Corinth? We are not saying of course that the Holy Spirit is not wanting to change the whole situation there. Of course, He wants to change the whole situation, but we are talking about the basis upon which the Holy Spirit commits Himself. It is a very, very important thing to get clear.

The church at Jerusalem might be legalistic. It might be highly bound. It might be lacking in full vision, but it was still the church at Jerusalem, nothing less and nothing more.

The church at Thyatira might even have a Jezebel in the midst, but it was still the church at Thyatira. The church at Laodicea might be wealthy, knowledgeable, full of activity, spiritually blind, poverty stricken and naked, but it was still the church at Laodicea. It was the one church, and this is a very, very important point. Some years ago I read a little statement I have never forgotten. It went like this. Never try to understand *the* church through the churches, but always seek to understand the churches through *the* church. That may not mean a lot to you just now; it will perhaps later in these studies.

The Church is One

The whole point is this: the church is one. It is absolutely one. It is indivisible because it is Christ. There is only one church. The fact that the name of a locality is attached to it is just simply that you happen to be a resident there.

When I go to New York, I am not a member of the church in Richmond visiting the church in New York. I am in the church. There is only *the* church. When I am here, I am in the church in Richmond; when I am in New York, I am in the church in New York. What I am doing when I am in a plane I do not know. But the fact of the matter is there is only one church. It is a question of where you are a resident.

Let us put it in New Testament terms. Supposing you were living in Antioch, then you were in the church in Antioch. If you moved to Jerusalem, you were in the church in Jerusalem. If you moved to Ephesus, you were in the church in Ephesus. If you moved to Rome, you were in the church in Rome. If you went from Jerusalem to Antioch you were just a member of the family. You were not a member of the Jerusalem church, but you were a member of the family. It was not so many little molecules, so many little entities all with a circle around them, local churches sort of pushed together. It was only one church divided just by the fact of where you lived. It is as simple as that. It is so utterly simple once the Holy Spirit reveals it to you.

In seeking to introduce this matter, I am saying that in the New Testament times, they did not face the complex problem that we face today in the twentieth century because there was just one church. Maybe there were Judaizers, maybe there was

Nicolaitanism, maybe there were false teachers and all the rest of it, but there was only one church just simply according to where you lived, and everyone knew that.

Supposing this place was Laodicea and we thought we would send a brother to Pergamum. They receive him. He comes from the church. *The* church in Laodicea is sending him to the same church in Pergamum. It is not the Laodicean Church sending him to the Pergamum Church. It is just the one church. It is just a question of where you live in a geographic locality. It is as simple as that.

The Early Christians were Cast on the Lord

When the believers were first gathered together, they were simply cast upon God. They did not have any big organisations, theological seminaries, Bible colleges or anything else; they were simply cast upon God and were taught to respond and obey the Holy Spirit so that the headship of Jesus Christ could be operative in their midst from their very first days. Thus if the apostle Paul went off and left them, they had to learn from the very beginning to look to Christ as their Head and their Lord by the Holy Spirit and find out what His way was. They were so cast upon God they learned to depend upon the life that was within them, and all the ministries, the functioning and the gifts were manifested, recognised, and appointed as time went on. Thus we can say that Christ continued to move and express Himself through His members on earth, through His body on earth. We have many terms for the church in the New Testament, whether it is body or members or house or temple or bride or church. It is the same thing.

Today there are Many Churches in a Locality

Today we have a very different situation. In any given locality, especially this one, there are any number of churches. I know one small Danish town with thirty-six churches. I dare say if we count up, we would find there are many more. That is the problem we have today; it is a far more complex problem. We have in this area alone National and State churches. We have denominational churches, interdenominational churches, and nondenominational churches. Then we have other groups, sectarian groups, exclusive groups and any number of others. Some are existing only for the propagation of certain aspects of truth. Some are there to bring us into certain kinds of spiritual experience. They call it the testimony. They say, "This is the testimony we have, the thing we are upholding which God has raised us up to give." Others look upon themselves as merely a means of reaching unsaved people, thank God for that, but it is only a means of reaching unsaved people, that is all. It is a kind of evangelistic agency. We are told that we should not desert such groups because it is a big pond in which we can fish. Some are unsound and erroneous using the name Christian merely as an appendage; for instance, Christian Science, Unity School of Christianity, and Christadelphianism. These things are using the name of Christ when in actual fact they have no part with Him at all. There are other groups that are sound, but are dead. As soon as you step in you feel the lifelessness of them.

You may hear a good little message as far as soundness goes. You probably could not pick any holes in it, but it is lifeless.

Others still have a measure of real life and real power which makes us more confused than ever. If they were all dead it would be a very simple proposition, wouldn't it? But when we find some groups full of life and full of power, that is our problem. What are we to do? The Lord is still blessing; the Lord is still saving; the Lord is still educating there. There is often some fellowship there and friendliness in varying degrees in different places. What are we to do? All of these groups in any given locality are built in some measure on the unity of the faith and of the knowledge of the Son of God rather than the unity of the spirit.

Two Unities

There are two unities. There is the unity we are arriving at, we are told in Ephesians 4:13: "Till we all attain unto the unity of the faith, and of the knowledge of the Son of God." But we are told in the same chapter, Ephesians 4:3: "Giving diligence to keep the unity of the spirit in the bond of peace." You cannot keep something you do not have. If you want to keep a dog, you must first have a dog, then you keep the dog. You cannot keep a nonexistent dog, can you? If you have a dog, then you would be diligent to keep the dog.

"Give diligence to keep the unity of the spirit." The very fact that we keep something means we have got it. So the unity of the spirit is something every child of God is born into, but the unity of the faith and of the knowledge of the Son of God is something that we are progressing toward. Now nearly all of these groups have made the unity of the faith the basis of fellowship. For example: "Have you seen the matter of baptism? You haven't? You can't have fellowship. You can come to the meeting, but you can't be right in." Do you see what I mean?

"Have you had the second blessing? If you have not had the second blessing, sorry. We will do our best to get you into it. But if you haven't had it, sorry, you are out." It is that kind of thing. Do you believe this, do you believe that? You are investigated as to exactly what you believe. You can go sit at the back, but you are not permitted to take any part or have any part in it at all until you have come into that experience or followed that method or something else.

I am perhaps not putting it too clearly, but that is the way most of these groups are built. They are built upon the unity of the faith and that is something none of us will ever all see eye to eye over until we are in the glory and then we shall all see eye to eye at last.

When we put a circle around ourselves we have a membership and then we give the right hand of membership, the right hand of fellowship. Once we have a membership, you are either in or you are out. Many of you young ones would never notice that when you go to a place like that because you sit in a congregation like you would sit here. You listen to the speaker and that is all right, but you do not know what lies behind it. There are many places that you would not be permitted to take part at the Lord's table unless you have been confirmed. You cannot take part unless you have had a certain ceremony, however believing they are. That is not so in every case, but in many cases. It is the same with baptism. In many groups, you will not be permitted to take the Lord's table unless you have been baptised by immersion as a believer.

Born into the Family of God

Now that is what we mean by all these groups being built upon the unity of the faith and of the knowledge of the Son of God and not on the unity of the Spirit. The fact is this: you may have only been saved an hour ago, but you have the unity of the Spirit. Thank God for that. You may be like a little baby newly born, in your first year spiritually, you may only have uttered one single word spiritually, but you are in the unity of the Spirit because you are born into God's family.

The basis is simply this: if you are in the family you are in with us. We cannot help it. We may not even like you, but what can we do? If God has brought you to birth, we have to accept the fact. Do you understand? So we are to receive one another as Christ has received us. How did Christ receive me? He did not receive me as a fully-fledged devoted servant of the Lord or something like that. No. How did He receive you? Did He receive you as someone who is a devoted, sanctified Christian? No. He received you as a miserable sinner who could not save himself, who could not do a single thing for himself. God accepted you as a sinner, saved by His grace. That was the lowest level on which He could bring us in.

Receiving One Another by Grace

We are saved by grace, and now you and I are to receive one another on the lowest, common denominator which is sinners saved by grace. We are not just sinners, but sinners saved by grace. Are you a sinner saved by grace? Well, my dear brothers and sisters, we cannot do anything about it; you and I belong together. You may not like it, but we are together because He has received me as a sinner saved by grace, and He has received you as a sinner saved by grace. You must accept me as a sinner saved by grace. I must accept you as a sinner saved by grace, not as a wonderful apostle or prophet or teacher or gifted child of God. But I must receive you as Christ received me. That undercuts a lot of the troubles we have in fellowship, doesn't it, a lot of these reservations we have about one another? You see we are all so adept at receiving one another on a basis other than the one on which Christ received us.

There may be someone here who has been saved for fifty or sixty years. You have been a child of God all those years and you have been going on with the Lord for all those years. Along comes someone who just got saved, a child just saved. Do you know he has as much right to be here as you have? He has, hasn't he? It is not because someone has gone on so long with the Lord that now the Lord says he or she is acceptable. He still accepts a person on the same basis as the day He received you the first time as a sinner saved by grace. So we are all together.

This situation we face, which I have said is so complex, is tragic because we have rent the unity of Christ by membership and by many other means. We have put little circles around certain numbers of us and said, "we are the elite," or "we are the agreed ones on this" or "we see this" or "we have experienced that." Now we put a little circle around it and say, "All of you are welcome to come and sit in the meeting but we are it. We are always out for an increase of our membership, if you would just go through the right channels."

Membership in the Lamb's Book of Life

I remember when I was first saved, I thought I was in the family of God. I was a Baptist and I remember my pastor approached me and said, "Isn't it about time you joined the church?" I remember looking at him in horror and saying, "Mr. So-and-So, I thought I was in the church." He said, "Oh, of course my dear boy, you are in the church. Of course, you are, but we live in the twentieth century." I said, "What has that got to with it?" He said, "You see, we have an organisation now. We have got to have it because we are in the twentieth century. Of course you are in the church, but you have got to join it." I asked him to show me in the Scriptures where you join the church once you are in it, but he could not.

Well, I naturally thought: he is my pastor, a dear man of God, a widely used servant of the Lord, so I accepted it and I was in. Do you know what I had to do? Two people had to come to see me at home separately to listen to my whole history. They wrote it all down and went back to the church and read the whole thing out in the church and took a vote on it. I went in on a two-thirds majority vote!

You all laugh, but that is Baptist Church procedure. I think, "What must the Lord think about going through all that kerfuffle?" I was received by the Lord as a sinner, saved by grace. Of course, they are seeking to protect themselves. Nevertheless, do you understand what it does? It cuts out those who have been saved by God and possibly includes someone who has not, who is clever enough to go through the whole investigation. The membership of the true church of God is the Lamb's book of life.

The situation, I must say, is a hopeless one humanly speaking, a situation of hopeless division, hopeless contradiction, and in many cases hopeless rivalry. Even when we sit under a banner, "All one in Jesus Christ," you know very well, if you have been on the inside of some of these things, the rivalry that goes on behind the banner.

Added to our confusion today is the World Council of Churches and the Second Vatican Council. Why does this add to our confusion? It is because here we have people who are not born again believers preaching and teaching the vital importance of unity. On the other side we have people who are born again believers justifying the tradition of divisions. Think: we have people who are not born again believers taking Scriptures and expounding Scriptures. I heard one of the [1]South Bank Theologians, a bishop, give the most magnificent address from the Bible on John 17 and Ephesians 4. I was sick inside because I thought if only some of our evangelical leaders could give the same message. This message is the right message amongst the wrong people.

Justifying Traditional Divisions

We had our annual evangelical convention within this town and a very well known brother, a blessedly used brother, a dear brother came, and he spent the whole evening justifying the traditional divisions among Christians. This is the hopeless

---

1 South Bank Theology was a discussion of moral and theological reform of the Anglican church in th 1960's which some Anglican's considered liberal. See *Oxford History of Anglicanism Vol. 4*

situation we are facing. We have the right people justifying the traditional divisions, and the wrong people preaching the vital necessity and importance of Christian unity, the unity of the church. In this town, for the first time, the Roman Catholics go to the Presbyterian Church. Think of it.

Yet what do the true believers do? We belong to and hide behind the World Evangelical Alliance, which justifies our divisions. We are told it is all right so long as we do not allow middle wall petitions to grow too high so that we cannot shake hands over the top. This middle wall of petition that we are told not to let get too high is a middle wall that Christ paid His blood to abolish. I for one think it is a terrible thing to talk about allowing a middle wall to remain, a wall which has been done away with by our Lord Jesus Christ at tremendous cost. We hide in the fact that we have a united, interdenominational, evangelistic campaign, and we have things like Keswick and other things. We say, "Isn't that good enough? Isn't there an expression of Christian unity there?" But this is the question you must ask yourself: Is that Biblical? I want you to ask yourself the question: Is it Biblical? It is all very well to say there are evidences there, but is that what the Lord really wants? For one week out of the whole year we all gather together and shake hands and have a united communion service and then we all go back to our various little groups. Is that really what the Lord wants? Is that New Testament? Now that is the problem which I hope you understand.

God Will Never Admit Defeat

The answer is this and we shall be dealing with this much more fully, but here is the answer in just a few sentences. We believe, by the grace of God, that the Lord will never admit defeat over His original purpose concerning His church. Let me say it again: The Lord, we believe, will never admit defeat over His original purpose concerning His church, and its expression and function on the earth during this age. Let me say it again: There are many evangelicals who would hide in the fact that something is being done up there in the invisible, ethereal realm which no one can ever see. They tell us that somehow or other something is happening up there, and that this church is without spot or blemish. Is this wholly Biblical? I say, the Lord will never admit defeat over His original purpose concerning the church and its expression on earth during this age. For the church expressed in time and locality is the workshop of God for the church universal and eternal. If the Lord cannot get that, He cannot really get the materials He needs for the eternal building.

Have the Gates of Hell Prevailed Over the Church?

So we will look at some scriptures. Matthew 16:18: "And I also say unto thee, that thou art Peter, and upon this rock I will build my church; and the gates of hell shall not prevail against it."

What does the Lord mean? If we look at the situation we have today we must say truthfully and honestly before God that the gates of hell have prevailed. What did the Lord mean? Does He not suggest that He will never admit defeat? Never! It is unbelief on our part that sides with Satan in this matter and says, "It shall never be." We need the Spirit of faith to come upon us so that we rise up as a man and say, "This thing is going to be, and hell cannot stop it! Our risen, glorified, enthroned Head is the One who is doing the work by the Spirit. That is what we stand for.

The Lord said in Ephesians 5:27: "That he might present the church to himself a glorious church, not having spot or wrinkle or any such thing; but that it should be holy and without blemish." Has He given up this idea? Is He going to let it go?

The Condition in the Corinthian Church

1 Corinthians 1:9: "God is faithful, through whom ye were called into the fellowship of his Son Jesus Christ our Lord."

Was there ever a situation more hopeless than the situation at Corinth? Was there ever a situation, if we had been in it, that we would have said: "This is just so awful that God has departed"? Immorality, carnality, law suits, divisions, factions, the exercise of gifts like so many babies, so that even the unsaved people coming in said they were mad. Don't you think if you had been in Corinth you would have suffered indescribably seeing it all? Don't you think you would have been tempted to leave them altogether and start something new? But what did the apostle Paul say? "Look here, those of you who say, 'I am of Paul,' you are the people who have seen. You have to leave this wreck and you have to start something again in a new way based on the teaching the Lord has given me." No he never did. Do you know what he said?

He said, "God is faithful through whom you have been called into the fellowship of His Son." God will do it.

Now if God could do it with Corinth, don't you think He could do it with this mess in the twentieth century? Do you think God is now unfaithful? To what have you been called? To what have I been called? To what has every child of God been called? Have we been called to another fellowship? Have we not all been called into the fellowship of His Son Jesus Christ our Lord? Therefore, is it not just as true that God is faithful, and he will see the thing through? Isn't that true? Oh, I am only just mentioning this because in the weeks ahead we will take it up and look at it a little more clearly with greater simplicity.

The Lord said so beautifully in Isaiah 46:10b: "My counsel shall stand, and I will do all my pleasure." The Lord is going to do this. We believe therefore that before the Lord Jesus comes, if only in a remnant, there will be an expression throughout the earth of His original thought and concept that His purpose in and for the church in this age will be carried by His grace to a glorious fulfillment and consummation. Do you know where I find my scriptural basis for that? In this wonderful word in Revelation 19: 7: "Let us rejoice and be exceeding glad, and let us give the glory unto him: for the marriage supper of the Lamb is come, and the bride hath made herself ready."

The Latter Glory of the House

What is the point of the book of Haggai? Is it there for archeology? What is the point in that little book of Haggai, that dusty little book all about building, and construction, and recovery, and completion of the house of God. I will tell you what it is there for. It is there for us that we might understand what it means when it says, "Yet once, it is a little while, and I will shake the heavens, and the earth, and the sea, and the dry land; and I will shake all nations; the precious things of all nations shall come; and I will fill this house with glory, saith the Lord of hosts...The latter glory of this house shall be greater than the former" (Haggai 2:6b–7, 9a).

Away with this idea in some quarters that the church is going to end up in some bankrupt, vacuous, empty wreck. That old, counterfeit prostitute that rides on the scarlet beast will end up a vacuous, empty, old wreck; but the bride will not. If only in a remnant, a tiny remnant all over the world, the Lord is going to do this. That is why we have Zechariah 4:6: "Not by might, nor by power, but by my Spirit, saith the Lord. Who art thou, O great mountain? Before Zerubbabel thou shalt become a plain; and he shall bring forth the top stone with shoutings of Grace, grace, unto it."

The Top Stone is Christ

The top stone is Christ, and the top stone shall be brought forth with shouts of grace, grace; it is the coming of the Lord. The house is absolutely built according to plan, according to the design so that the top stone is fitted into position. That needs the cooperation in utter devotion and faithfullness of every child of God. It means that you have to get your loyalties clear. People speak a lot about loyalty. Loyalty to this thing, loyalty to that thing, loyalty to this servant of the Lord, loyalty to that servant of the Lord.

What do they mean? I have only one loyalty and it is to the Lord Jesus Christ.

The Work of the Holy Spirit

We have to be sons of Levi in this matter. We have to take the sword and destroy everything else in utter loyalty to Him. We have got to go through. *We have got to go through.* Now, don't you fear because the Lord is going to go through and that is the whole point. He is going through, so do not get frightened as if we have to barge our way through the whole thing like a kind of spiritual bulldozer. What we need is faith. The Lord has done it. All He needs is for a people to rise up and say, "This thing shall be!" Why? Because of the finished work of Christ, because of Pentecost, it shall be. If the early church was glorious, the latter church will be more glorious; not because it is more universal, or more in number, but because it has cost more. That is what it needs, a people that will rise up in faith and say, "This thing shall be," and it shall be because the Lord has done it. Not by might nor by power but by His Spirit He will do it. That is the bulldozer; could we want a better? The Holy Spirit, blessed be His name, is the bulldozer of God, the dynamite of God; He will blast a way through if only He finds faith in you and me. We are not trying to put over something, trying to get something done.

Too costly, isn't it? I would rather have a nice life in the country; retire to the twittering birds and the sunsets than be in this business. But thank God, the Lord is in this thing and He is going to do it. So that is why we are here. The great thing is this:

and here is the one and only reason. You are here because you are in Christ. It is simple as that.

If you were in anything else, it is Christ plus—Christ plus baptism, Christ plus second blessing, Christ plus tongues, Christ plus the second coming, Christ plus this experience of everything. You are just here because you are in Christ; that is all. That is the reason. You are in Him and I am in Him, therefore we are not going to be divided. We are going to stay together. So long as you are in Him and I am in Him and we are living here in Richmond, we are together. If you do not like me you can go to live in Edinburgh. That is the best way out of it. Then you can still be in Christ, but we are parted by five hundred miles. Then we can write nice letters to one another. But while we are here in Richmond, you are in Christ and I am in Christ. We are together and we have got to find a way through it. May God help us to understand just a little more of what this means.

Shall we pray:

Beloved Lord, we need Thee; we all need Thee. Oh, we pray that Thou wilt give us some real spiritual enlightenment as to what we are doing here. Oh Father, only Thou canst do that. Wilt Thou by Thy Spirit really translate into our hearts and minds the truth that we have been talking about this evening. Lord, get us clear as to why we are together, clear as to what Thy objective is, Lord. Oh, help us in this thing, and do it for Thy name's sake. Now we are going to praise Thee, Lord, for what Thou art going to do. Whether with us or with some other company Thou art going to do it in the end. Praise Thy name. So Lord, together we just bow before Thee and worship Thee. We look to Thee, Lord, that in all that lies ahead there may be more and more for Thyself in us all as we go on together. We ask it in the name of our Lord, Jesus Christ. Amen.

2.
The Headship of Christ

Ephesians 1:22–23a

And he put all things in subjection under his feet, and gave him to be head over all things to the church, which is his body.

Ephesians 5:23

For the husband is the head of the wife, as Christ also is the head of the church, being himself the savior of the body.

Colossians 1:18

And he is the head of the body, the church: who is the beginning,

the firstborn from the dead; that in all things he might have the preeminence.

1 Corinthians 11:3–5a

But I would have you know, that the head of every man is Christ; and the head of the woman is the man; and the head of Christ is God. Every man praying or prophesying, having his head covered, dishonoreth his head. But every woman praying or prophesying with her head unveiled dishonoreth her head.

John 16:13–15

Howbeit when he, the Spirit of truth, is come, he shall guide you into all the truth: for he shall not speak from himself; but what things soever he shall hear, these shall he speak: and he shall declare unto you the things that are to come. He shall glorify me: for he shall take of mine, and shall declare it unto you. All things whatsoever the Father hath are mine: therefore said I, that he taketh of mine, and shall declare it unto you.

1 John 2:20, 27

And ye have an anointing from the Holy One, and ye know all things...And as for you, the anointing which ye received of him abideth in you, and ye need not that anyone teach you; but as his anointing teacheth you concerning all things, and is true, and is no lie, and even as it taught you, ye abide in him.

Matthew 23:8–10

But be not ye called Rabbi: for one is your teacher, and all ye are brethren. And call no man your father on the earth: for one is your Father, even he who is in heaven. Neither be ye called masters: for one is your master, even the Christ.

What Are We?

Now we come to the second of the series we are taking on the question we have asked: "Why are you at Halford House?" In one way these times are all related. They come out of the preceding times and therefore all of them are of a piece. "Why am I at Halford House?" Is it just an evangelical church? What are we here?

Are we a kind of Open Brethren Assembly that allows sisters to take part or are we a kind of evangelical church whose minister wears normal clothes and is called Mr.? Or are we a mission to those who have some kind of trouble in their background? What are we? Are we the propagators of an especial truth or an especial type of spiritual experience? Supposing some leading evangelicals approached us and asked us why we are here at all? Why don't we join one of the other groups, a sound denominational group? Or if we do not like denominationalism, why not join an interdenominational or a nondenominational group? If we do not like organisation maybe we can join the Quakers or the Open Brethren. We sought to introduce this series last week in this way.

One Church in a Locality

We have spoken about the problem that confronts us as Christians today. In the New Testament things were very simple and straightforward. They were clear-cut. When a person became a child of God, they were immediately known to be within the family of God. In every locality the family of God, those who have been born again of the Spirit of God through the preaching of the gospel, gathered together, and they were called the church. There were never two churches in one locality. It was as simple as that. So you were either in it or you were not in it. It was exclusive of all, however good or decent or Biblically knowledgeable, who were not born of God, but it included every single one who professed an experience of God's saving grace.

The problem we confront today is a very complex one. In any given locality, there are hundreds and hundreds of churches—

national and state, denominational, interdenominational, nondenominational, fellowships, missions, gospel halls—many of every kind. Our point is: what should we do? All, in some measure, are organised, institutional, or a sect. Nearly all are built on the unity of the faith rather than the unity of the spirit.

The Lord's Original Purpose Will Be Accomplished

Now I would like to take up the last point we made. You will remember that we said we believe that the Lord will never be defeated over His original purpose for and in His church. At the end of this age, if only in a remnant worldwide, He will once again recover something of the nature of the church and express something of His power, His life and His glory. (You will have to take up this in another course, extra to this time, about the history of the church in which we trace the successive movements of the Spirit of God as He has sought to recover something which has been lost.) But suffice it to say that we believe that there will be an expression throughout the earth of His original thought and concept and that His purpose in and for the church in this age will be carried by His grace to a glorious consummation.

We find it all understood in the little phrase in Revelation 19:7: "Let us rejoice and be exceeding glad, and let us give the glory unto him; for the marriage of the Lamb is come, and his wife hath made herself ready." "...hath made herself ready."

Now this needs the cooperation in utter devotion and faithfullness of every single one whose heart is set on the Lord. We must give our loyalty without any shadow of reserve. We must give our loyalty, first and foremost to Christ, and, if by giving our loyalty to Christ first and foremost, other loyalties to people and to things are shattered; they must be shattered!

There is a lot of talk about loyalty to things. I have often had it put to me like this: why do you leave the sinking ship? Only rats leave the sinking ship. I will never leave the ship while the captain is still at the wheel, but if (a thing that should never happen) the captain gets away in the lifeboat, I am going with him. If the captain gives up the ship, I am not staying on that ship.

Let me put it in New Testament terms: if the candlestick is removed from the church at Ephesus, I am going with the candlestick. Let me put it in terms that our dear brother Watchman Nee put it when he said: "There came a time in the history of the people of God when the ark of the covenant and the tabernacle got separated. In one place there was the ark of the covenant with a few priests who worshiped the Lord, and in the other place there was the tabernacle with all its furniture and accessories with most of the priests. He said, "Where would you have worshipped?" Then he said this: "In days of decline and departure follow the ark of the covenant and forget the tabernacle, for the ark of the covenant represents the sovereign presence of the living God.

Taking the Ground of the Body of Christ

Now, those of you who are always here know we do believe in loyalty. We believe in loyalty to one another. We believe in loyalty to that which God has shown us and given us. The faith once and for all delivered—for that we must be prepared to die. We believe in that loyalty with all our hearts, but we do not believe in any loyalty to man or things which takes the place or precedence over loyalty to Jesus Christ. In my estimation it is almost blasphemy to even suggest that we should be loyal to other things if it means disloyalty to Jesus Christ. Thus we have been led by the Spirit of God to take the ground of the body of Christ.

Last time we put up the various points that people might say in answer to the question: Why are you at Halford House?

Friendliness and fellowship
Freedom of the Spirit
Good spiritual food
The measure of Christ, or more of Christ there
"I was saved there"
"I think it is the will of God that I should be there."

Some of these things are good things, but we said really, they were all wrong. In the end we put at the bottom the two words: In Christ. I am there because I am in Christ. I do not want Christ plus a denomination. I do not want Christ plus organisation as such. I do not want Christ plus anything; I just want to be there because I am in Christ, and I want to open my arms to every other person who is in Christ whoever they are, whether Catholic or Protestant. I just want simply to open my arms to them if they are in Christ. I want to receive them as Christ has also received me—in Christ.

Let me put it another way, a more technical way. It means that we take the ground of the body of Christ. How are you and I in Christ? What does it mean? Because you and I are in Christ, we are in the body of Christ. He is the Head; we are the body. We are in the body. The body is joined to the Head. It is part of the Head; it shares the name of the Head.

All the members of my body are sharing the name of Lance Lambert; no one else's name, only mine. They are in my body, and that is why the Scripture speaks of you and me as members of Christ, members of His body. You can see that in 1 Corinthians 12:12, Romans 12:4–5, 1 Corinthians 6:17–18. You will find it in a number of places, "members of Christ, limbs of Christ, parts of Christ." That is what you are if you have been saved by the grace of God.

So we have been led by the Spirit of God to take the ground of the body of Christ. We do not believe that there is any other excuse for meeting separately than that ground; for to meet on any other basis would be another division. Therefore, if we can find ground upon which we can receive every believer as a believer and not have to ask a whole list of questions, that is ground that ends division.

If we are to leave things, surely we must find something that is not itself going to be split and split and split. It is like the old story of the Quaker meeting that broke up into two and then the two broke up again, and then it broke up again, and finally there was only the old lady and her chauffeur. As she was on her way to the meeting she said, "You know, all the world is a little queer save thee and me, and even thee is a little twisted."

That is how we can end up. Once you start making truth only the basis for fellowship or spiritual experience, other than the initial one of new birth, you end up by thinking everyone is peculiar.

The Headship of Christ Over His People

We are going to deal with one point now, which is perhaps the most fundamental of all. What does it mean to take the ground of the body of Christ or to take church ground as sometimes we put it? First, it means the headship of Jesus Christ over His people by His Spirit. It is the absolute headship of Jesus Christ over the church or to the church.

First, I want you to notice the term *body*. I am sure even if you have only been a Christian for a week or two you have surely noted that the term *body* comes again and again in the New Testament with reference to the church. Now notice that term *body*. A body is only a living, functioning, developing, growing thing when it is joined to a head. But if you want to conduct an experiment you can cut your head off and you will soon find out. Bodies die the moment they are separated from the head because for the body to be a living, functioning, operative thing it must be joined to the head. However, it must be more than that. It must not only be joined to the head, it must be obedient to the head. If there is the slightest trouble in our nervous system from the brain to the body, we are paralyzed. We can have the most beautiful head in the world with the finest features in the world, we can have the most beautiful body in the world with the finest physique, but if there is anything wrong between the brain and the body, between the head and the body, there is paralysis. There is no point in the body. The head and the body belong to each other; they need each other. We think of a head and the body as a person. You are all here and there is not one of you here, think of it, without a head. Furthermore there is not one of you here without a body. Every person in this room has a head and body joined together.

The Vital Factor of the Head

In Ephesians 4:15–16 we read this: "But speaking truth in love, may grow up in all things into him, who is the head, even Christ; from whom all the body fitly framed and knit together through that which every joint supplieth, according to the working in due measure of each several part, maketh the increase of the body unto the building up of itself in love."

What I want you to understand is this: it talks about the body developing and growing and being built up in love of itself. But how does that come about? It comes about when each member of Christ grows up into Him as Head. The Head is the vital factor in the functioning of the body. The headship of Christ is the vital factor in the function of the church. There can be no development, no functioning, no growth, no movement, no manifestation, no expression of Christ in the church until it knows the headship of Christ in experience. You may only have to know it very, very simply, what it is to bow the knee to Jesus Christ as Lord; not just one but all of us, everyone ready to accept the authority of the Lord Jesus Christ in any issue over any matter. But until you have got that there can be no functioning of the church.

Holding Fast the Head

Again in Colossians 2:19 it says, "And not holding fast the Head, from whom all the body, being supplied and knit together through the joints and bands, increaseth with the increase of God."

"Holding fast the Head"—not the body. Holding fast the Head from which the whole body increaseth with the increase of God. There can be no functioning, no growth, and no building together, no real fellowship, what the Bible calls fellowship—which is not just chatter—there can be none of that until we know the Head, until we hold fast the Head, and each one has a personal relationship, a clear cut open supply line to the Lord Jesus Christ.

I want you to note very carefully one important point. We do not experience the church by trying to hold fast the body. We do not come into an experience of the church by saying, "I must hold fast all these dear people. I must try to get close to them. I must try to agree with them. I must try to somehow move with them." This is the idea that is so prevalent; this is where the Exclusive Brethren went right off the rails. Everyone held fast the body but forgot the Head, and gradually the whole body veered away from the truth until now they are in the saddest plight it is possible to be in.

You will never ever, however young you are or however old you are, experience church life or fellowship by trying to hold fast the body. The way it comes is by holding fast the Head and then we discover the body. As we keep absolutely clear our link with the Lord Jesus Christ as King and Master we then find the body. Isn't that true? Every time you take a step in obedience, haven't you found yourself closer to the church? It is true. Every time you have an issue in your life, isn't it true you have a battle with the saints? You can say this about them and that about them, pull them up on this and pull them up on that. They are wrong here and they are wrong there, teachings are too long or this is too bad and this and that, when we have an issue with the Lord. But suddenly, when you settle the issue, you feel so free with all the saints. Why is that? It is holding fast the Head. When you hold fast the Head, you find the body. It is as simple as that.

All Authority Centred in the Head

What do we mean by this word *headship*? Why does the Bible speak of Christ in these scriptures as Head of the body? What does it mean? We associate a person's mind, their will and their intelligence with their head. When we say, "So-and-so has a mind," what do we think of in our imagination? We think of their head. Or if we say, "So-and-so has got such a will," we think of their head. If we say, "A person has got a thick head," we mean they are not too intelligent. We say a person is hot-headed, that is they have a strong will, and their feelings will carry them through into something. It is the head we think about in these things.

The Bible takes this term, this symbol head, and it speaks of or it means that all authority, government, leadership, and teaching are wholly centred in the Person of our Lord Jesus Christ. That is why we read that scripture, "Don't call anyone a Rabbi, even if he is an apostle. Don't call him Rabbi so-and-so. Don't call him Father so-and-so. The Lord Jesus Himself said it. Do not call him Master (see Matthew 23:8-10). He is plain Mr. in the sense that he is just a brother in the Lord. You are all brethren. You have only one Teacher, you have only one Master, and you only have one Father.

We must get this quite clear. In this matter, when we talk about the headship of the Lord Jesus Christ, all of this is wholly centred in Him. There is no other authority in the church other than Jesus Christ. There is no other government in the church other than Jesus Christ. There is no other leadership in the church other than Jesus Christ. There is no other teaching other than the teaching of our Lord Jesus Christ. Let us get that quite clear.

The Supremacy and Centrality of the Lord Jesus Christ

The headship of Christ also speaks of the supremacy and centrality of our Lord Jesus Christ. He is Lord of all. Now the Head is supreme in the body in the sense that it is the headquarters of the body. It is, as it were, the telephone exchange of the body. Everything comes into the Head; everything goes out from the Head. The Head is the operative centre. The Lord Jesus Christ is absolutely supreme and absolutely central. He is the heart and the centre of everything.

Anything that cannot give the Lord Jesus Christ the place which God has given Him has got to go. Now that is the reason why there is difficulty in Christian circles. The enemy has engineered all of us into such a position that we are unable to let go of all that would have to go in order for the Lord Jesus Christ to have the place which God the Father has given to Him. We have got to be absolutely clear and definite in this matter. Anything which cannot give the Lord Jesus Christ that place of absolute supremacy and centrality has got to go. That is the standard by which we judge everything.

What does the Word of God say? Colossians 3:11 says, Christ is everything and in everyone—supreme and head. If there is anything in which He cannot have the glory, He cannot have His place, it must be wrong. It belongs to another world; it belongs to another kingdom. It belongs to another sphere. You must note in Scripture that it is not only Head that comes under this term *headship* but King and Lord. These are titles that the Lord Jesus is given.

The Lord Jesus Enthroned and the Holy Spirit Released

When we say that taking the ground of the body of Christ means the absolute headship of Jesus Christ, someone will say to me: "How is that practical? We cannot see Him and with our physical ears we cannot hear him. You say there is to be no other authority, no other government, no other leadership, no other teaching other than Jesus Christ. Isn't that rather mystical? Isn't it rather abstract, rather vague?"

Now this is just the point. The Father has enthroned the Lord Jesus Christ at His right hand with all power and authority as King of kings and Lord of lords. And the moment the Lord Jesus took His position, took His seat at the Father's right hand, that moment the Holy Spirit was released. You will remember the Lord Jesus said, "If I do not go the Holy Spirit will not come, but if I go I will send Him unto you" (see John 16:7). The moment the Lord Jesus sat down on the throne of God, with all authority and all power in heaven and on earth in His hand, that moment the Holy Spirit was released. What is the work of the Holy Spirit? The work of the Holy Spirit is to make practical, concrete and real the position, the authority, the mind, the will and the life of Jesus Christ to the church.

What happened on the day of Pentecost? Suddenly one hundred and twenty units of a congregation became one hundred and twenty members of the body. How did it happen? The Holy Spirit came. What happened when the Holy Spirit came? He came like the sound of a mighty rushing wind, and then it was like fire, a furnace of fire; a ball of fire fell on the one hundred and twenty. But what happened? Suddenly the fire split up; it was one fire, but as it were, a tongue of flame settled on each single member of the one hundred and twenty. There was one Spirit in one hundred and twenty; one life in one hundred and twenty; one Head made real to one hundred and twenty. The one hundred and twenty became one hundred and twenty members of a single body.

What happened? The next moment the apostle Peter stood up and all the eleven stood up with him. What were they all doing? Only one of them spoke, but they felt so much with him that they all rose up with him and they all remained silent, all eleven of them, and Peter did all the preaching. They stood the whole time he was standing; they felt so much a part of him. What had happened to these quibbling, divided, disillusioned, disappointed disciples? These were the men who would always argue: "Who should be first?" If it had been just a year before, they would not have stood up with Peter and some of them would have said: "Who does he think he is?" If John and James' mother had been there, she would have been starting trouble: "My sons are better than that Peter any day."

You know the scripture; I am not just joking, it is true. They were always quibbling about position. They were not really together. The only Person who kept them together was the Lord Jesus pouring oil on troubled waters all the time; but after the day of Pentecost something happened; they were all one. What happened? The Holy Spirit came. Oh, someone says, "That means power; that means fullness." Yes, of course, it means power and fullness, but those are subsidiary things. I am not saying they are not vital in a personal and corporate way, but what I am saying is this: the Holy Spirit came to make real to the church the position of our Lord Jesus Christ enthroned at the right hand of God far above all principalities and power so that this body becomes invincible.

Now it is the measure in which the Holy Spirit has freedom to make real the position, the authority and the mind and will of Christ in us, that measure in which He is free to do this, which is the measure in which we know the life and power of God. Every single revival in the history of the church, every great movement of God in the history of the church, which has recovered anything for God, has begun with the re-enthronement of the Lord Jesus Christ by the Spirit of God. Every single backsliding, every single departure, every single decline has begun with the dethronement of our Lord Jesus Christ.

Not by Might nor by Power but by My Spirit

That is why we have read the scripture in John 16:14 about the Holy Spirit: "He will take of the things of mine and declare them unto you." What are the things of Him? His position, His authority, His power, His incorruptible risen life. Think of it! You can even take it for your body, for your mind if you have faith. That is a personal thing. It is not the first thing by any means, but oh the glorious little second things that there are, the little fruits that fall by the way from the tree that is laden in this matter of the coming of the Holy Spirit. I am simply saying to you that the Holy Spirit came to make real the invincible, incorruptible authority, power and position of our Lord Jesus Christ. If you and I are going to see anything happen in this world in the end time, when darkness is going to cover the whole earth and when those evil, foul spirits are going to create a suffocating atmosphere of vileness and wickedness, it will not be by might nor by power but by His Spirit that the house of God shall be completed, that the bride will have made herself ready.

So let's get this clear. If you and I want to know the mind of Christ, if we want to know the will of Christ in any given situation, if we want to know the authority of Christ in any given situation, if we want to know the position of Christ—and we are in that position, don't forget that—then the Holy Spirit is here to show us. He is not up there; He is here. He is in this room. He is here in this place. He is in this company. He is here and His job is to make real all of that to us. So do not say that it is mystical, or very abstract.

The Holy Spirit Transmits the Mind of Christ to the Church

The history, at least in a very poor and failing way, of this little company, has been simply that we have heard the mind and will of God again and again. We are, after all, the stupidest crowd in the world that God has brought together. It is absolutely true; we are just a terrible crowd, but we have learned one simple lesson: that the Lord Jesus Christ is Head and Lord of us all and that His mind can be transmitted to us by the Spirit of God. We may be the dumbest crowd in the world, but if we have an ear for the Spirit, then the Lord, as it were, will do everything He can for us.

This clears the ground of all those substitutes, all those things which become substitutes for the headship of Jesus Christ which so effectively frustrate its practical outworking. Christianity, Christian circles and evangelical circles are cluttered up with things, New Testament things and non-New Testament things, which effectively paralyse and frustrate the outworking of the headship of Jesus Christ, so that with all the devotion in the world the Lord cannot have His way. We may be devoted but He cannot have His way. What are those things? They are human selection and appointments. When I think of what goes on behind the scenes, when I think of nomination and election and all the things that go on, it is incredible—councils, committees, boards, etc, etc, etc.

Substituting Any Head in the Place of Christ

I remember when I was first saved, I heard a brother say, "If you put twelve men's heads together, you will produce one board." It is so true. I remember he was once asked how the work that he was in was run. "What kind of committee do you have?" He said, "Oh, we have an extraordinary committee. It is limited to three. It is always in session; they are always one and they get everything done—the Father, the Son and the Holy Ghost."

The fact of the matter is this: all these things, whether New Testament or non-New Testament, if they become—and I underline if—if they become substitutes for the practical outworking of the headship of Christ, they are wrong. Congregational business meetings, Presbyteries, New Testament set-ups, sparkling with their rigidity, if they substitute their heads for the headship of Jesus Christ, they are wrong.

More than that, the point we need to make and make emphatically is this: These things, whether they are right and scriptural or not, if they become a substitution for the headship of Christ's government, for Christ's mind, for Christ's will, they are not only utterly wrong, they are perniciously evil. That may shock some of you, but I say it before God; they are not only utterly wrong, they are perniciously evil. Why? They not only frustrate Christ, they contradict God's order and they substitute man's thoughts for God's thoughts. Therefore, I say they are perniciously evil. If there are lots of things one day on which I have to be put right when I stand before God, I am sure this will not be one of them. There is no greater pernicious evil amongst evangelicals than this utter frustrating of the will and mind of

God. You can have zeal, and devotion, and love, and sacrifice on the part of so many believers, but at the heart of it everything is paralysed. To me, the devil's main objective is, by all means, to divorce the church from her Head and so to frustrate God's mind and paralyse the body.

The Practical Outworking of Christ's Headship

Much Prayer

To me, the headship of Christ in its practical outworking means much prayer; not many words but a spirit of prayer. Why? Because that is the way we find the mind of Christ. As we get on our knees and bow our heads to His head, as we inquire of the Lord, as we seek His face for wisdom and understanding as to what His mind is, He gives it through His Word, by His Spirit. It gives us an understanding of what it means. It means much corporate prayer. Now I do not mean by that just a meeting where a lot of petitions are made. God bless so and so in Indonesia and God bless so and so in Brazil. God bless the big meeting up in London tomorrow night. God bless Annie's leg and heal it. These may be right, but the fact of the matter is, that is not the kind of prayer I am talking about. I am talking about the kind of prayer meeting which is a throne room meeting with God where we are in the holiest place of all, and we are inquiring of the Lord as to what His will is, and what His mind is. If the Lord is Head and if the Holy Spirit has been given, surely He means for us to be practical and concrete in our attitude. Surely He means for us to get on our knees and say, "Lord, what should we do about this situation?" It is not that we all put our heads together and we will then do the aggregate of what we all feel. But what does the Lord say and can He transmit this feeling of His will through us all. I believe that means there must be in any company that takes the ground of the body of Christ a refusal to do anything without first inquiring of the Lord—and don't we know it!

If there is one thing the Lord is more jealous of than anything else it is if we do anything without first asking Him. You can go through the whole Old Testament and you will find that borne out in incident after incident and also in the New Testament. If we just do things because that is the way they are normally done, if we just do it because that is the traditional institutional thing to do, if we do it even because we find it in the Word and we think that is the way we ought to do it, we make a mistake.

We have made those mistakes, haven't we? What we say from our own history is that we have learned. We once had a really good New Testament set up, and you could not pick holes in it; but it was all wrong. There are other things we have done as well. The point is the Lord wants a people who are in touch with Him, not just having a little blue print they can hang up on the wall. Every time anything goes wrong just go look at the blue print and say, "Now then." That is not it. The Lord wants a people in touch with Him so He can communicate with them, so He can put over to them what is really in His mind. There has to be a refusal to do anything without first inquiring of the Lord. Further to that there has to be a readiness to pray and to wait on the Lord until we are certain that the Lord is showing us all what His mind is.

Waiting

Waiting—that is the headship of Christ. In other words, if the Lord says, "Go," we go. If He says, "Stay," we stay. If He says, "Wait," we wait. If He says, "Do nothing," we do nothing. We just obey. Do you believe that the Lord Jesus Christ is alive? You do. You are a Christian and you believe He is alive? Do you believe that He is King of kings and Lord of lords? You do. Do you believe, as the scripture says, "He is at the right hand of God the Father, the Majesty on high"? You do. Now tell me, do you not think the Holy Spirit, whom He has sent, would make real in us altogether as a company corporately what that will and mind is? Don't you think that? Think it out. Why should any man stand in the place of Christ and tell us what he thinks? All right, we do not mind anyone making his or her suggestions. Everyone is free to make their suggestions and give their opinions providing everyone will bow to the absolute lordship of Jesus Christ in the final and ultimate analysis.

Executive Action

I believe also this matter of the headship of Christ not only means much prayer, but it means executive action can be taken in the name of our Head. It is wonderful. Executive action can be taken in the name of Christ so that the will and Word of God are realised. In other words, woe betide any company that comes on what we call the ground of the body of Christ if they do not know in the end how to take executive action in the name of Christ; they will be undone. That is why the Lord said, "Thou art Peter, and upon this rock I will build my church; and the gates of hell shall not prevail against it. To thee, Peter, I have given the keys of the kingdom: and whatsoever thou shall bind on earth shall be bound in heaven; and whatsoever thou shall loose on earth shall be loosed in heaven" (see Matthew 16:18–19). In other words, Peter, if this church is to be built in spite of your shaky, unrocklike, impetuous nature, you have the keys to it. Do you think the Lord could entrust such as we with the keys? But if the church is not being built upon the rock, it is because we are not using the keys, and the only people who can use the keys are those who are on church ground. Keys are not given to anyone else. They are given to the church.

Matthew 18:19–20 says, "Again I say unto you, that if two of you shall agree on earth as touching anything that they shall ask, it shall be done for them of my Father who is in heaven. For where two or three are gathered together in my name, there am I in the midst of them." This is executive action in the name of the Lord Jesus Christ.

Greater Works Than These Shall You Do

Look at John 14:12: "Verily, verily, I say unto you, He that believeth on me, the works that I do shall he do also; and greater works than these shall he do; because I go unto the Father."

The Lord fed five thousand in one place; He fed four thousand in another place. He preached the Sermon on the Mount to enormous multitudes, but He could count the converts, the real converts. At the end of His life there were one hundred and twenty. However, on the day of Pentecost Peter stood up with the eleven and they preached—as one great theologian has put it—one of the most terrible sermons in history, quite disjointed, and three thousand people were saved on the spot and baptised. "Greater works than these shall ye do" (John 14:12b).

Listen to this: "Because I go unto the Father and whatsoever you shall ask in My name that I will do that the Father may be glorified in the Son. If you will ask anything in My name that will I do" (see John 14:13–14). Executive action.

The New Man—Part One and Two

Acts 1:1: "The former treatise I made, O Theophilus, concerning all that Jesus began both to do and to teach."

Have you ever noticed that? "Began both to do and to teach." In other words, the writer of the Acts is saying, "Now look here, I am going to write the second part of my work. The first is called the Gospel according to Luke. Now I am going to write the second part."

The former was what Jesus began to do, so the inference is that Acts is what Jesus continued to do and to teach. But how did He continue to do and to teach? He was not there. He did it through His body. So Luke and Acts are two volumes of one work and we could entitle them: The New Man, Part One and Part Two. Part one is Jesus Christ the Head, and part two is Jesus Christ the Head and the body. Simple. Executive action.

Now I will give you two references out of very many in the book of Acts of executive action. One is when Peter said with John to the man who was lame: "Silver and gold have I none; but what I have, that give I thee. Rise up in the name of Jesus Christ of Nazareth" (see Acts 3:6), and he rose up and leapt.

The other occasion was when they had been put in prison and came out miraculously and went to their own company and found them praying. What a prayer meeting they had! It was executive. They did not say, "Please, please." They said, "Lord, stretch forth Thy hand with signs and wonders in the name of Thy holy Child Jesus" (see Acts 4:24–32). And the place was shaken, and they were all filled with the Holy Spirit. That is evidence of executive action.

The Right Place of Man

Finally, we need to see the right place of man in the headship of Jesus Christ. We have said a lot about what is wrong— human selection, human appointment, counsels, committees, boards. Some might say, "It is a little extreme, isn't it? He has wiped the whole board clean. The lot is gone. What are we going to have?" Of course, I have tried to put "ifs" in. I said, "If they substitute, they become substitutes for the headship of Jesus Christ."

What is the right place of man in the headship of Jesus Christ to the church? The headship of Jesus Christ is direct to every single believer. You do not have to have a mediator; you do not have to have a priest or anything else. You can go directly to the Lord Jesus Christ.

Listen to these wonderful words: "Ye have an anointing." Where is the anointing? On the head of Jesus Christ. You have an anointing from the head of Jesus Christ, from the holy One, from His head you have an anointing. His anointing on His head has come to you and dwells in you. You do not need anyone to teach you. Now does that mean we can give up teaching? That we can despise anyone who has a teaching ministry? No, of course not! But it means that you do not have to be told what is right and wrong; you have the Holy Spirit within you; you have an anointing within you. You have a direct link with the Head. You do not have to depend on a kind of clergy to tell you this is right and that is wrong, so you just close your ears and say, "I will not think about it. If they say that is right, it is right. If they say it is wrong, it is wrong." Now that is quite wrong. You have an anointing. No one needs to teach you. You know what is wrong. If you look at it in the context you will see it immediately. You know what is error; you know what is false; you know what is antichrist. Individually, there is the direct Lordship of Jesus Christ to every one of us.

Every Man Holding Fast to the Head

If you look at Colossians 2:19, you will see that it is personal. "Every man," it says. "Not holding fast," speaking of the man who has a fleshly mind which is in the singular. He does not hold fast the Head. Every one of us has a direct holding fast to the Head, and we must go directly to Him. We must not get our direction from a church. We must get our direction from the Head and test it in the church. That is why if you do not ask us to bring something for prayer to the company, we do not bring it. So do not think that you can be very humble and modest and say, "Well, I do not want my little matters brought to the church. If they think about it and want to mention it that is good." We never will because we respect your right. If you do not want to test it in the church, we will never bring anything of yours to the church. But if you come and ask us, we bring it to the church, but we will never say anything to you until we are sure that you have something from the Lord because we are not here to direct you as to what you should do. We are here so that you can test out whether what you have from the Head is right. It will save you from mistake or collapse.

The Corporate Place of Man

What is the place of man corporately in the headship of Christ? Let's say this clearly. Whilst His headship is direct to every believer, it is not vested in every believer. There is a difference. It is direct to every believer, but it is not vested in every believer. In other words, there are certain ones in the church who are equipped, qualified, chosen of God and appointed by God that are the ones in whom the headship of Jesus Christ is vested, expressed. They represent the government of the Lord in the church. Now let's just look at some scriptures very quickly.

I Timothy 5:17: "Let the elders that rule well be counted worthy of double honor [e.g. *double wages*], especially those who labor in the word and in teaching." Let those elders that rule well; mark the word *rule*, not advise. Rule is a strong word.

I Timothy 4:14: "Neglect not the gift that is in thee, which was given thee by prophecy, with the laying on of the hands of the presbytery." That is the eldership, the elders, the presbytery.

I Peter 5:1–3: "The elders therefore among you I exhort, who am a fellow-elder, and a witness of the sufferings of Christ, who am also a partaker of the glory that shall be revealed:

Tend the flock of God which is among you, exercising the oversight [*e.g. ruling, supervision*], not of constraint, but willingly." Don't be pushed into it. That rather puts a bomb on the forced modesty that sometimes you find in some quarters. "...according to the will of God; nor yet for filthy lucre," do not do it for cash, "but of a ready mind; neither as lording it over the charge allotted to you, but making yourselves ensamples to the flock."

Hebrews 13:17: "Obey them that have the rule over you" may that sink into everybody, "and submit to them: for they watch in behalf of your souls, as they that shall give account; that they may do this with joy, and not with grief: for this were unprofitable for you."

So one day the Lord is going to ask the elders of each company about everyone who was in the flock.

Elders and Deacons

Now you see straightaway that there are certain men chosen of God, prepared by God and appointed by God that are called elders. In the local church they are called elders. You will find bishops, and there was always a plurality of bishops in the New Testament church. You can see from the scriptures that elders and bishops are synonymous. In Philippians 1:1, he writes to the church of God which is in Philippi with the bishops and the deacons, elders and deacons. So in the local church this headship of Jesus Christ is vested in the elders or bishops.

Apostles and Prophets

Amongst the churches it is vested in what we call apostles or prophets. Often people say to me, "But surely apostles have died out. Didn't they go out with the first church?" Yes, of course, the twelve apostles are unique. And then we have Paul who is unique. Some people say he should have been the twelfth in place of Judas and it was a mistake to put Matthias instead. That may or may not be, but how do you explain scriptures like Revelation 2:2: "And ye have done well that ye have tried those that call themselves apostles and are not." Everyone knew the twelve apostles so how could people go around saying, "We are apostles," if there were not many more apostles? How do you explain Timothy who was an apostle? How do you explain Silvanus who was an apostle? There is such a thing as apostolic authority even today. It is what we call an authority that is wider than the local church.

Now Peter was both an apostle and elder. He says: "I also am a fellow-elder," yet he was an apostle. John called himself "the elder" yet he was also an apostle. He was an elder in the local church and an apostle when he went out of it.

The Importance of Spiritual Character

What we can say is this: it is absolutely essential that such men have a truly spiritual character. They must be chosen of God, appointed by God, apprehended of God, prepared and trained by God, and finally empowered by God.

There are two things that are essential in any who take any small part in the headship of Jesus Christ in its actual practical outworking in the church, eldership or any other way. The cross must be the principle of all their service and if a man does not know something of the brokenness of the cross, he cannot be an elder or anything else. The second thing is that he must know the

Spirit. These are two essentials. Otherwise our heads are in the place of His head.

The Cross

If the cross does not work, it will be our head instead of His. We cannot help it. It is a natural thing to use your head. I know that goes against a lot of what you are told at school, because it is the natural thing for all of us to use our heads. However, unless we know the cross we use our heads in a wrong way. We are all the time putting our heads in the place of Christ. We mean well, but we cannot help it. It is only when the cross breaks us. We still use our intelligence, we still use our mind, but we bow to the headship of Jesus Christ. We are His bondslaves.

The Spirit of God

But it is not just the cross. It is a terrible thing to be just negative, broken, ready to bow, ready to submit, and yet not have the power of the Spirit of God to know the mind of God. By the Spirit we know the things of God and the deep things of God. To those who exercise eldership or apostleship or anything else in this way, they have got to know the Spirit of God in an increasing measure. That is why everyone who was chosen was full of the Spirit.

The book of Acts is the perfect illustration of all that I have said about the headship of Jesus Christ from beginning to end. It is our enthroned Lord who deals with Ananias and Sapphira and everyone else. The book of Acts is a marvellous story and picture of the headship of Jesus Christ to the church, and everywhere the result: the church—churches everywhere over the whole Roman

Empire, right in Rome itself. What has happened? Rome has collapsed and the church is still here. Isn't that amazing!

Two Testimonies in the Church

The Laying on of Hands

There are two testimonies. One is the testimony of the laying on of hands. Whenever we lay hands on someone, we express the headship of Jesus Christ. That is what we do when you are baptised. We put hands on you and that means you are under the headship of Jesus Christ. You are in the body under the Head. It is a lovely picture. For instance, whenever we lay hands on someone and they go out, it means they are part of the body under the Head. Even though we say, "Good bye," yet they are in the same body. They are not leaving the body; they are going from the body to the body. You are going with the Head. Even when people are sick and the elders lay hands on them, this is what it means. They are under our risen Head who is anointed to do anything, even drive out sickness if necessary.

The Sisters' Head Covering

The other testimony is the ladies wearing hats. I will not go into it, but it is all there in the Word and you can ask the Lord all about it. It is a testimony to this very thing we are talking about, the headship of Jesus Christ. And as one brother once said, "Once you have seen it, you would wear a million hats piled one on top of the other, it is so glorious."

A Letter by Evan Hopkins

Listen to this: it is from a private letter written by the late Reverend Evan Hopkins who was the founder of Keswick. You will remember that Evan Hopkins was minister here in Richmond a hundred years ago.

I have a vision of the kind of meetings that will be held in the near future. God's people will meet together, not primarily for the outpouring of the Holy Ghost on the world, as for the manifestation of His power in and through His church. They will meet together not so much with a view of realising their union in Christ as of seeking their unity in the Spirit. They will come together not only in one place but really and indeed in one accord. Then there will not only be union, that is oneness of life, but the unity oneness of heart. Let that point be reached and the demonstration of Holy Ghost power will be seen. They will come together seeking the Holy Spirit, not as if He were an absent Lord, but as One verily in the midst, One who is waiting to put forth His power. This is the vision I seem to have of what is not far distant of the character of the meetings that will be held in connection with prayer for a world-wide revival. The Holy Ghost, who is in the church but is grieved and hindered in His work because of the lack of this unity amongst believers, will then put forth His power through the church and work mightily among the unsaved.

There are just a few copies of that. Do you know to whom it was written? It was written to a lady who lived in a house just opposite here and it was written to her when she was in Richmond, when she was in a big conference in the north of England, Mrs. Penn-Lewis. Isn't that amazing? Thank God! I often wonder whether Mrs. Penn-Lewis prayed for the old school of art when she saw the people coming up the road and coming in here. It is amazing.

Shall we pray:

Beloved Lord, Thou knowest all the weakness in our life together as a people and in us individually in this matter of Thy headship, but Lord, we do want Thee to be Lord. We know from the little experience we have had that the greatest glory, and power, and life, and fullness comes from being in touch with Thee and doing Thy will and being obedient to Thyself. Oh Lord, teach us Thy way and above all work in us so much that we are ready to do Thy will, ready truly to do Thy will together. So Lord, we thank Thee. If there is anything that has been hard to understand on the part of any, oh Father, by Thy Holy Spirit reveal and illuminate. We ask it in His name. Amen.

3.
The Heavenly Church

John 3:13, 31

And no one hath ascended into heaven, but he that descended out of heaven, even the Son of man, who is in heaven...He that cometh from above is above all: he that is of the earth is of the earth, and of the earth he speaketh: he that cometh from heaven is above all.

1 Corinthians 15:47–49

The first man is of the earth, earthy: the second man is of heaven. As is the earthy, such are they also that are earthy:

and as is the heavenly, such are they also that are heavenly. And as we have borne the image of the earthy, we shall also bear the image of the heavenly.

1 John 4:17

Herein is love made perfect with us, that we may have boldness in the day of judgment; because as he is, even so are we in this world.

(... as He is, even so are we in this world.)

Hebrews 3:1

Wherefore, holy brethren, partakers of a heavenly calling, consider the Apostle and High Priest of our confession, even Jesus. (... partakers of a heavenly calling)

Hebrews 12:22

But ye are come unto mount Zion, and unto the city of the living God, the heavenly Jerusalem, and to innumerable hosts of angels. (... ye are come to heavenly Jerusalem)

Philippians 3:20

For our citizenship is in heaven; whence also we wait for a Saviour, the Lord Jesus Christ. (... our citizenship is in heaven)

Ephesians 1:3

Blessed be the God and Father of our Lord Jesus Christ, who hath blessed us with every spiritual blessing in the heavenly places in Christ. (... every spiritual blessing in the heavenly places in Christ)

Ephesians 2:6

And raised us up with him, and made us to sit with him, (... and made us to sit with him) *in the heavenly places, in Christ Jesus.*

We are not going to go through them, but you ought to make a note of the approximately thirty-three times that the phrase kingdom of heaven is used in Matthew's Gospel.

Galatians 6:15

For neither is circumcision anything, nor uncircumcision, but a new [creation]. (New is the word I want you to underline.)

Ephesians 2:15

*Having abolished in his flesh
the enmity, even the law of
commandments contained in
ordinances; that he might create
in himself of the two one new
man.* (... a new creation,
a new man)

Ephesians 4:24

*And put on the new man,
that after God hath been created
in righteousness and holiness
of truth.*

Colossians 3:10–11

*And have put on the new
man, that is being renewed
unto knowledge after the
image of him that created him:
where there cannot be Greek
and Jew, circumcision and
uncircumcision, barbarian,
Scythian, bondman, freeman;
but Christ is all, and in all.*
(From this we learn this new
man is a corporate person.)

Romans 16:25

*Now to him that is able to
establish you according to
my gospel and the preaching
of Jesus Christ, according to
the revelation of the mystery
which hath been kept in silence
through times eternal.*
(... according to the revelation
of the mystery)

Ephesians 1:9–11a

*Making known unto us the
mystery of his will, according
to his good pleasure which
he purposed in him unto a
dispensation of the fullness of
the times, to sum up all things
in Christ, the things in the
heavens, and the things upon
the earth; in him I say, in whom
also we were made a heritage.*

Ephesians 3:3

How that by revelation was made known unto me the mystery, as I wrote before in few words.

Ephesians 3:9

And to make all men see what is the dispensation of the mystery which for ages hath been hid in God who created all things.
(... the stewardship or dispensation of the mystery)

Colossians 1:26–27

Even the mystery which hath been hid for ages and generations; but now hath it been manifested to his saints, to whom God was pleased to make known what is the riches of the glory of this mystery among the Gentiles, which is Christ in you, the hope of glory.

Colossians 2:2–3

That their hearts may be comforted, they being knit together in love, and unto all riches of the full assurance of understanding, that they may know the mystery of God, even Christ, in whom are all the treasures of wisdom and knowledge hidden.

I want, if the Lord wills, to cover two very important points. We asked ourselves the question: "Why are you at Halford House? Why am I at Halford House?" We have sought to introduce the matter and have given a short answer as to what we believe. Then we have said, because of that it requires all those who really are devoted and faithful to the Lord, to give their complete and utter devotion to Him and to give their first and foremost loyalty to Christ, even if it means foregoing loyalty to things and people.

The Headship of Christ

We have spoken about taking the ground of the body of Christ. In practical terms, last week we dealt with the first point. This means the absolute headship of the Lord Jesus Christ in and over the church by the Holy Spirit. That is why we always pray about things in all levels of the work, with all its weaknesses, and failures and breakdowns. We do seek always to get before the Lord and seek Him, whether it is the elders or all of us together, whether it is this aspect or that aspect. Whatever it is, we try to go to the Lord about every problem. All our mistakes made in the history of this assembly, which we could spend the whole evening talking about because they are so illustrative and instructive, have been made because we did not first inquire of the Lord. Someone would come up with a bright idea, which we all fell in with or we went on a majority vote, which was the classic mistake at the very beginning. Therefore we threw out voting altogether from that day to this. All our mistakes have come because we did not first inquire of the Lord.

We have said that we have taken the ground of the body of Christ. We are in Christ, and because we are in Christ we are members of His body, and that is the ground we have taken.

The Church is Heavenly

The second point I want to make may at first seem to be obscure, but believe me it is anything but obscure. The church, His body, is a heavenly thing and is therefore inexplicable on the natural level. I repeat it again: to take the ground of the body of Christ means that His body is a heavenly thing; it is a heavenly matter in a heavenly position with a heavenly life, with heavenly resources, and it is therefore inexplicable on the natural level. At first that might seem very obscure, but I think as we deal with it you will see that it goes to the root of very much in modern Christianity.

The church is the heavenly body of her heavenly Head. You cannot have a heavenly Head and an earthly body. Neither can you have an earthly head and a heavenly body. They must be one. We know that our Head is in heaven and that He is from heaven. What a mysterious word that is in John 3:13 where it says, "And no one hath ascended into heaven," *[i.e. no fallen man has been able to attain heaven]* "but he that descended out of heaven," *[that is our Lord Jesus Christ, the Son of man]* "even the Son of man, who is in heaven."

Now this was said of the Lord at a point when He was on earth. How, therefore, was He in heaven at that point? The Lord Jesus said, "... who is in heaven." His present position was in heaven.

You have it again in verse 31a: "He that cometh from above is above all."

Again in 1 Corinthians 15:47: "The first man is of the earth, earthy *[that is Adam and all of us. We have all come out of it. We are of the earth, earthy.]* The second man *[Jesus Christ]* is of heaven."

The Lord Jesus is of Heaven

The Lord Jesus Christ came from heaven and is of heaven. His body is therefore, as He, heavenly in nature and character. In other words, this is precisely what it means in that somewhat wonderful but mysterious comment in I John 4:17b: "Because as he is, even so are we in this world." No one can relegate "in this world" to the eternal future. In other words, He is from heaven; we are of heaven. If we have been born, we have been born from above. That is why it is a new birth—born again, born anew, born from above, born of the Spirit; and because of that we are in the kingdom of heaven. We have received our Lord Jesus Christ who is the Man from heaven and we have been joined by the Spirit of God to Him, so we are one.

A New Creation

We can put it this way: Christ and His body, the Head and the body together constitute the new man, the new creation. That is why we have those references about the new creation. Circumcision or uncircumcision do not mean anything now. It does not avail anything nor is it of any value; but rather it is a new creation. What a wonderful word that is in II Corinthians 5:17–18a: "Wherefore if any man is in Christ, he is a new creature: the old things are passed away; behold, they are become new. But all things are of God."

I think that word has brought a lot of children of God into condemnation because it says, "Wherefore if any man is in Christ, he is a new creature." But if you look in the Revised Version you will find in the margin an alternative rendering which is just as accurate and just as possible as "he is a new creature." And it is this: "Wherefore if any man is in Christ there is a new creation." I love that because that is precisely true. There is no new creature in my old flesh. No good thing dwelleth in me, naturally. My old flesh has been crucified. But in Christ there is a new creation. He is the new creation; He is the new Man, and He has begotten me and begotten you again. We are of Him; we have a heavenly life and a heavenly Head. The church's character, the church's resources, and the church's life are all heavenly. Even the position of the church while on earth is in heaven. That is why we read this word in Ephesians 1:3: "He has blessed us with every spiritual blessing in the heavenlies." You find it again and again in the scriptures that the position of the church is in the heavens.

The Church is in the Heavens

Here we are on earth, yet our position is in heaven. That is not something to do with the future when we go through the pearly gates, so called. That is an altogether misunderstanding of the way the term heaven is used. It is not a future place. It is a sphere, a realm into which you and I are introduced now. One of the clearest hallmarks upon which I believe we can be completely dogmatic, one of the clearest hallmarks of that which is the genuine work of God, the work of the Holy Spirit, is always its distinctive heavenliness and spirituality. Therefore you can judge everything by this. You can go to this meeting, go to that meeting, the naïve can be swept away by the claims that are made about everything else, but in the end it is the distinctive spirituality and heavenliness of that work or of that ministry which is the hallmark of whether it is of God. You can be quite sure that anything that has the earth in it is dangerous. Anything that is a mixture or completely of the earth is dangerous. Be careful of it. Nor does it take more than a superficial reading of the New Testament to see how the use of this word *heavenly* or *of heaven* or *in heaven* is connected with the life and resources of the church. Wherever you look in the New Testament you will discover that this is so.

What is Heavenliness?

But what do we mean by heavenliness? That is the question. What do we mean by heavenliness? I think it is all summed up by the little phrase we often hear: "Too heavenly minded to be of any earthly use." And although we all laugh at that, in fact it goes to the root of the general idea of what heavenliness is. In the general Christian's mind, certainly in the world's mind, heavenliness means that you are abstract, vague, mystical or impractical. Some people say, "Well, you know it is a very heavenly character that so and so has got." What they mean is they cannot wash dishes. That goes to the root of it.

I remember once asking about a certain group from a very tough missionary that we all knew as Tiger, and I have never forgotten the explosion there was. "Too heavenly minded to be of any earthly use!" That is all I got. I could not find out anything. I had to go to other sources to find out what was meant by this. But the word *heavenliness* as we use it, actually does not appear in the Scripture. But the word *heavenliness* just means simply "of heaven, out of heaven, from heaven, characterized by heaven." So when we speak of the heavenliness of the church we mean that her life, her character, everything is formed out of heaven, sustained from heaven.

Now if you consider the church in this way there are one or two things we can say very simply. The church is conceived in heaven, which is the first thing. She is born from heaven, governed from heaven, or out of heaven, sustained by heaven. She has a growing, heavenly character. Her consummation is in heaven.

This simply describes and comprehends everything about the church that you and I know or have experienced. Where was the church conceived? She was conceived in the heart of God, in the mind of God from before times eternal in heaven. It was a heavenly conception. Where was she born? On the day of Pentecost by the Holy Spirit coming out from heaven. She never came out from the earth; she came out of heaven. How is she governed? By the Head. Where is the Head? At the right hand of the Majesty on high in heaven. How is she sustained? She is kept by the power of God. Where does the power of God come from? Through the Head by the Holy Spirit. It is heavenly. She has a growing, heavenly character. In other words, she is being conformed to the image of Him who died to save her. Where is the consummation going to take place? The consummation is going to take place in heaven. We are going to be caught up. Think of it! It began in heaven, and it came from heaven with the Holy Spirit on the day of Pentecost. It is governed, developed, protected, anointed from heaven, and one day, glory, it will be caught up by the power of the Holy Spirit to meet with her Lord in the air and then there will be the marriage supper of the Lamb. Where? In heaven. It is not down here; it is up there. From whence shall it appear? It is from whence He shall appear. It is also from whence she shall appear. Where does she come from? I saw the holy city, the new Jerusalem coming down out of heaven. She is going to be caught up to be with her Lord and then she will appear with Him in a universal way coming to and upon this earth.

The Church—An Enigma to the Natural Man

Thus there is about the true church that which is wholly inexplicable to the natural man. It is a mystery to him. The man in the street just cannot understand the church. (Now I am not talking about what we call the church; I am talking about the true church.) It is an enigma to him. He cannot understand it; it is a mystery. He asks a few questions and gets a few replies and he is more mystified than ever. The thing is an absolute mystery to him from beginning to end. It is inexplicable to him because it is wholly outside of his realm and sphere. He is of the earth earthy. Because this thing is in heaven, he just cannot understand it.

The fact is that the true church is concrete and practical; it can be seen. Away with this idea of the invisibility of the church. It can be seen; it can be handled; it can be touched. It is human and located. That is the church on earth. The fact that it is so concretely expressed, so tangibly expressed only makes it more inexplicable to this world. If only the whole thing was a mystery, if only it was completely abstract and vague and all up there, but the fact is they see something. They see cohesion, they see unity, they see a love, and they see a practical outworking of something. Oh, they see the failure and the break down as well, but they see some things they cannot explain. It all seems so ordinary, so human, and very much like any other fellowship or club or society or organisation, yet it is an enigma because its source, its fountainhead is somehow not the same.

The True Church—As Inexplicable as Christ

The easiest way to understand it is this: To the natural man the true church is as inexplicable as Christ was when He walked on this earth. Was Christ visible? Of course He was visible. Was Christ tangible? Of course He was tangible. Was Christ human? Yes. They said, "Isn't this the son of Joseph and Mary? We know Him. He's the carpenter." That was the enigma. If He had just been like Melchizedek without beginning and without end, just drifting in somehow, it would all have been much easier. But He was not. On one side He seemed to be so ordinary, just like the rest of us, but the next minute He was an enigma. He could feed five thousand men apart from the women and children. He could feed another four thousand men apart from the women and children. He could walk on the sea. He could raise the dead. That was completely inexplicable; yet the thing that made Him more mysterious and more of an enigma than anything was the fact that He seemed to be just like us. He had two eyes, two ears, a nose, a mouth and a body. He ate like us; He became weary like us; He slept like us; He cried like us, but who is He? He seems so heavenly.

Now the church is exactly, precisely that. She is to be felt and touched in the same way. She is to be known and seen in the same way and yet she is an enigma. Where does she get her resources? Where does she get her power? Where does she get her life? How is she governed? How do these people know when they say, "We do the will of God"? How do they find it out?

Well, you see, this is both the impact and the glory of the church. The church almost completely loses its impact when she loses her heavenly character, when she becomes explicable. The glory of the church is the fact that she is from heaven. She has a life this world does not know of; she has a Lord this world has rejected. She has a power that is beyond anything in this world.

"How did it come into being?" the world asks. Supposing they ask us how it came into being. Don't you find it difficult sometimes to answer? The more you know about the history of this company, the more difficult it is to answer. I always say, "Where shall we begin? Should we go back to Egypt? Should we go back before Egypt?" Shall we say, "We started with prayer gatherings"? Yet that is only the science of it. How did it begin? It was born somehow. Everything that is really of God is born of the Spirit. How can you explain that to the natural man? How can you explain that to the world? They say, "How did it come? There must be a human personality somewhere." Yes, there are human personalities, and that is what makes it even more inexplicable because they are there. Yet you can have other personalities and it does not happen.

How is the Church Governed?

"Oh," someone says, "how are you governed? Are you governed by bishops, or an archbishop, or a priest, or fathers or elders? How is it done?"

You reply, "Well, it is rather hard to say. We have elders, but we get on our knees and we ask God."

"You ask God?"

"Oh, yes."

"Of course, you are asking God about Aunt Fanny who has died and gone over."

"Oh, no, we are not asking about Aunt Fanny who has gone over to the other side. No, we do not do that kind of thing."

"Then what do you ask Him? You don't ask Him about practical things like carpets and gardens or whether you should do this or that."

"Oh, yes we do."

"How does God speak to you? Does He speak with an actual voice? Can you hear Him? Do you hear a voice suddenly like a loud speaker speaking in the middle of the room and saying, 'You shall do so and so?'" This is the very kind of thing that you know mystifies the world. "How do you hear the voice of God? How do you find the will of God?" You all talk about it, then avoid it by saying, "It is nonsense."

Hearing the Voice of God

I remember the time when Bill first came to work for us and I had a little talk with him. We thought it was the only honest thing to do. I said to him: "Now Bill, you do realise that you are not employed by us, don't you?"

"Oh, yes."

"You are employed by God."

"Oh, yes, yes."

Then I said to him: "The fact is you have to be very careful about this because it is God who is going to pay you your wages."

"Oh, yeah, yeah. If something happens, what do I do about it?"

"Well, you come and tell us and we will pray."

"Yes, yes," and he went off. No more was said. Every week he asked for the sum, and every week it was there. So he told us afterwards, "I thought it was just religious talk." (These are Bill's own words; we have witnesses.) "I thought it was religious talk," he said. "It is the way these Christian people talk; but they have it all down in the bank. Of course, they say they prayed, but they trot down to the bank, draw it out and give it to me."

Every time he asked for it we had it; until that famous occasion when he asked for three hundred pounds and it was not there. He came to me on Thursday morning, and by that time he had learned our phraseology, and said, "Has the money come?"

I said to him, "No. Strangely enough, it hasn't."

So he looked at me and said, "Oh."

So I said, "Listen, have you done the work right?"

He said, "I think so." Then he thought for a while and said, "Perhaps there are some screws that should have been put in here and there, and a latch that was wrong, so I will go and do that."

So I said, "You do it because God sees everything."

He said, "Do you think the money is going to come?"

I said, "When do you need it by?"

He said, "By two o'clock so I can get it into the bank by three o'clock."

"It will be here by two," I said.

By then there was a second post, and I thought, "Come on, Lord." The second post came and there was nothing but bills in it. Then at lunchtime we did not know what to do, so I said to them all (it was cleaning day), "We will go upstairs and pray." We went upstairs into the library and had a little time of prayer. Every single Christian on the premises went upstairs. I think there were about ten or eleven of us. Bill came through just after two and walked through the back door, past the front door mat up the stairs. When he got to the library door, he did not knock or bang on the library door; he just opened it, and then we heard it shut quickly. Bill told me later: "I have never felt so sick in all my life because I heard someone saying, 'Lord, we do not have that three hundred pounds. We have got to have it now.'"

He said, "I clutched my stomach. I have been sick many times through over drinking, but I have never felt so sick. I went down the stairs like a drunken man going from side to side, and said to myself, 'God, they do not have the money. They do not have the money. I have been trusting them and I thought they had the money. What am I going to do?'"

When he got to the bottom of the stairs, he saw there three hundred one pound notes. He was the one who came up and opened the door and said, "You can stop praying; here is the money." Inexplicable!

The amusing side of this is that he tried to explain that to his bank manager. His bank manager wanted to know if we were creditable people. "Oh, they've got no money," he said, but they trust God." So, that is when the bank manager said, "Oh, yes." But it is inexplicable.

How is the Church Financed?

People ask: "How is the church governed?" Look at it. How is it governed? Of course, outwardly you have certain things, but inwardly there is something else. It is the Lord Himself. How do you explain that to someone? How is it financed? "Oh," they say, "you must have a collection. If you do not have a collection you must have a lot of rich people." But when they get to know us, well then what? How is it happening?

I remember the first time we started the work here, a minister said to me: "Look here, you have got to be practical, Lance, because you have a mystical side to your nature." Now this was a very dear evangelical leader who said, "You have a mystical side to your nature; you have to be practical. You have got to have a collection or you will not get anything and the church will not get anything."

I said, "That is terrible to say that."

He said, "No, you will find out in time you cannot be all up in the air about this. God's people have got to be reminded." I was so annoyed with God's people at that moment, I said to him, "If God's people have to be reminded, I think God can do without their cash. I do not see that God wants their pennies; they can keep them. If the only way God can get you to give to Him and do His work is by continually shoving a collection plate under your very nose, I should think you might as well keep the cash. Go buy an ice cream with it. I am sure it would be of more value than dropping it in a plate for God."

Now I am not saying the collection is necessarily wrong, but the reason we do not have collections is because we believe there is a higher way. It says in the Word: "Don't let your left hand see what your right hand is doing" (see Matthew 6:3). In the collection plate not only does your left hand see what your right hand is doing but everyone else sees it. That is the idea behind it. That is the psychological idea behind the collection. The people feel shamed into giving something. You all know the feeling.

You nudge someone and say, "I don't have anything, can you lend me something?" It is because you cannot bear to let the plate go by. It takes courage to do it or meanness.

How is it financed? It is financed by the Lord. He said, "My God shall supply every need of yours according to His riches in glory in Christ Jesus" (Philippians 4:19). How wonderful it is when they say, "Where did you get your money?" My mother is always onto us about where we get the money. She is the best detective in the place, always trying to track it down. "Well, it must have come from so and so," she says. They cannot understand it. How does it happen?

I will never forget when my mother came back one day and said she had talked with Phyllis. Phyllis had said that there was a problem with the sink; it was blocked up. She put a wire down it and prayed about it. We wiggled the wire and the Lord did the rest. My mother was simply mortified. She did not know what to say because she did not know such people existed. It is inexplicable when you have Someone to fall back on who has promised to be absolutely faithful.

How is the Church Sustained?

Now on a more serious note. How is the church sustained? You think of the outward annihilation of the church in certain parts of the earth, and what happens? It surges back. It seems that the devil had dealt a deathblow to the church and wiped it out. Then suddenly you find it is there, and not only there, but there more strongly than it has even been in its history. The baptism of fire and blood has only brought it more truly into being.

Nero discovered that. The Roman Empire has long since collapsed, but the church has not. How is it sustained when so many other things have faded out and have been liquidated by autocrats or dictators? It is because it is from heaven.

How Does One Join the Church?

Then suppose someone says, "How do you join it?" How do you join the church? Can you explain that to the natural man? Of course, if you have a membership you can explain it straightaway just as you can explain finances if you have collections, and appeals and all the rest of it. If you do not have these things, how do you explain how you join the church? You say, "Well, you must be born of the Spirit."

"Are they cranks there? What does he mean?" It is inexplicable.

Now this is much more important than perhaps most of us realise. This that I have been talking about, whether a thing is explicable or inexplicable, is the tragedy of so much that goes by the name of Christ. It is so wholly explicable to this world. The natural man can understand entirely because it is like any other worldly organisation. How do you join it? Join the membership; get the right hand. Pay a little bit, look right, say the right things, and you will be in. In some set ups, get two people to sponsor you. That is what it virtually amounts to and you are in.

How is it run? Committees, councils, boards galore. It is entirely explicable. Everything else in this world is run by committees, boards and councils. It is entirely explicable.

How is it financed? We only have to look at some notices outside some of the churches to see: begging, groveling for money. It just makes it so explicable. The way it is organized, the way it is financed, the way it is governed, the way it is joined. It is just like any other society. What is the difference between that and a stamp collecting society or a bird watching club or some other club or society? It is run basically on the same lines. You have people who are elected officers, you have people nominated to take control, you have appeals when funds run low, and all the rest of it. Indeed, I might say some worldly organisations run their finances a good deal better than some so-called churches.

The Attacks of the Enemy

It is also this heavenly nature and character of the church which the enemy is continually attacking and assaulting. There are two ways in which he attacks.

An Earthly Counterfeit

The first is this: he seeks to create an earthly counterfeit, something which is wholly of this earth. It uses the name of God, the name of Christ, the things of God, the Word of God, and all the rest, but it is absolutely and wholly of this world. It has a form of Godliness but it denies the power thereof. It is humanly established, humanly formed, humanly governed, and humanly financed. That is one line of attack.

An Earthly Compromise

The other is what must concern us here the most. The other is to seek to bring down that which is heavenly to earth, into and unto an earthly level, to compromise it so gravely that it becomes a mixture, neither wholly of earth nor wholly of heaven. In this you will find nearly the whole of church history. What denomination, which began as a heavenly move of God, has not ended up on earth as worldly, as earthly as anything else. God is very practical on this, very, very practical. He says we are to serve the counsel of God in our own generation. I have absolutely no doubt at all that if we could all be here to watch and look at a meeting in one hundred years, if the Lord should tarry, we shall see the same thing happen here. No doubt about it. It is the earth-bound, earthward tendency in everything once it comes to the second, third and fourth generation. It loses its holy, heavenly character and then becomes a mixture. Little things are introduced that you and I do not even think about, it seems so legitimate, and so good, and so desperately needed. They are instituted and they bring the end. Few people see the end of a seed that is planted; they only see the need. I have no doubt about it. The same thing will happen here as it happens everywhere, but our point is today, the present, serving the counsel of God now in our own generation.

A Warning

We ought also to take careful note of this warning that we do not have to make it inexplicable. There are some Christian leaders in some groups who seem to think that because the church is heavenly and therefore inexplicable it is our job to make it inexplicable and mysterious. They sort of "heavenize" everything. There is a kind of singularity, a kind of peculiarity, and more unkindly we could say, it is eccentricity amongst Christians, which is wholly lamentable. Now when a person is odd before they were saved and it is a temperamental matter, the Lord often uses the oddness. But God save us from people who become odd because they have been saved. There are plenty of them. There are plenty of groups that get into that trap as well.

Now our Lord Jesus was not eccentric. He was not peculiar; He was certainly singular. But He was not peculiar; He was not eccentric; He was not one of these odd, queer birds. He was absolutely normal, flesh of our flesh, bone of our bone, as it were. We could understand Him, and that is the enigma. I don't find one of these mysterious, queer, eccentric types heavenly at all. I think, of course it can all be explained. They talk about hearing voices and seeing visions and I think they are a bit odd anyway.

When I meet someone who is absolutely normal and they start talking about hearing the Word of God and so on, then that is an enigma if I am a man in the world. He would say, "I cannot understand it; this man is so normal. He laughs like me, he cries like me, he sleeps like me, he walks like me, he lives almost like me in one way, and yet there is a heavenliness." Do you see what I mean? That is heavenliness. Now get that clear. You will never go wrong if you think of our Lord Jesus. If you ever want an example of heavenliness, it is the Lord Jesus. Think of Him and you will be preserved from all these weird, queer ideas that float around.

The Heavenly Head and the Heavenly Body

We have two or three illustrations of this. One of them is the book of Acts from Pentecost onwards. What is it but an illustration of something wholly inexplicable to man, heavenly in nature and character? You can see the church that came into being on the day of Pentecost. See how it moved through the book of Acts. It had failings and faults. They were all human beings, very much human beings, yet how inexplicable it is!

If we take the Gospel according to Luke and the book of Acts and entitle them "The New Man, Volume One, the Head" which is Luke, and "The Body, Volume Two," which is Acts, you have exactly what I am driving at. One is as inexplicable as the other—the heavenly body and the heavenly Head.

Of course, the other thing is the testimony in baptism. When we are baptised, we bear testimony to the fact that we are in something heavenly. We have been cut off in the waters of baptism. We have been cut off from the old, from the earthy. It does not mean that we do not have a lot of trouble with the old man or old woman, but the fact is that we are in Christ and that is the testimony, the glorious testimony.

The Body is an Organism

Now I am going to begin to talk about another principle, which is that the church—His body—is an organism and not an organisation. We will look at one or two Scriptures.

> *For even as we have many members in one body, and all the members have not the same office: so we, who are many, are one body in Christ, and severally members one of another.*
> *Romans 12:4–5*

From I Corinthians 12:12 right the way through we find there again this organism illustrated.

Speaking truth in love, may grow up in all things into him, who is the head, even Christ; from whom all the body fitly framed and knit together through that which every joint supplieth, according to the working in due measure of each several part, maketh the increase of the body unto the building up of itself in love.
Ephesians 4:15

It is something organic. We grow up into Him who is Head, and the whole body fitly framed and knit together through that which every joint supplies increases with the increase of God. It builds itself up. It is an organic thing.

In Colossians 2:19a: "Holding fast the head." You have the same thought here.

Now most evangelicals give lip service to the truth that the church is an organism. I know very few evangelicals who do not say, and very few Bible colleges where it is not taught that the church is an organism. Everyone agrees and they all give lip service to this, but it is in the practical outworking that there is contradiction, inconsistency and breakdown. The church is an organism, but when it comes to the practical outworking, it is the most extraordinary thing—everyone forgets it is an organism.

For instance, many evangelicals seem to feel that to be nondenominational in spirit is enough. You can even belong to a denominational church, but if it is nondenominational in spirit that is all that is required—just to be broad, and loving, and free and open. Others go further and would say, "Providing one is in a nondenominational church, that is all that is required. Denominationalism is the real blight, the real curse amongst us Christians."

Organisationalism

In fact, denominationalism is only the symptom; it is not the disease. Get this clear. It is only the symptom; it is not the disease. The disease is a very deep-seated thing indeed, and I would call it "organisationalism." That is the disease, and if you think about it every denomination has somehow evolved from organisation. As it has become more and more organised, more and more top heavy, it has died and become a set, rigid organisation. I am not saying God does not use it or God does not bless it or God does not save in such a thing. Of course He does; they are His children, where His children are found. But never mix up all the blessing and all the other saving activity of the Holy Spirit with God owning it. God may use it but He does not own it, and He will dump it one day. It will all go back to where it belongs, Rome. Birds of a feather flock together, and it will gravitate to its right and true centre.

You can have something that is completely nondenominational and yet as organised as anything which is denominationalism, and that is why there is no life there. So some people, particularly young people today, say, "What is the point of all this talk about recovery of the church and so on? We are in something which is absolutely New Testament." But it is dead as dead can be, and it is so heavy and so lifeless. Then what happens? We find again and again people leaving so-called New Testament groups and going to the other extreme because they say, "God does not seem to bother very much about whether it is New Testament or not."

The fact of the matter is that organisationalism, even if it is New Testament in pattern, is the disease. Anything that substitutes human organisation, however New Testament in appearance, for that which is organic—the work, the product of the Holy Spirit's energies and life—is what I call organisationalism.

Now it is an extraordinary fact that you only have to get twelve people together and they start to organise themselves. Some here can bear witness to this. (I was the archfiend in this.) There were only about sixteen of us gathered together and what do you think we did? We had an extraordinary meeting to elect officers. We gained ourselves a little membership and then we had officers. The Holy Spirit was so gracious; He brushed the whole thing aside. After that extraordinary meeting, although we had elected the whole lot, we never once took note of it. But the thing was in our lifeblood, in our very system, and it was impossible, as it were, to get it out of us.

This is exactly what happens. Think of the many so-called New Testament groups that have split up and been shipwrecked on this. Who is going to be leader? Who is going to be elder? Who is going to have this ministry or that ministry? Who is going to have this position or that position? What a caricature it is! They talk about the church, but they are not in it in experience. Potentially, of course, they are in it, but they are not really in it in experience. It is an extraordinary thing!

The Church—Not a Free-for-all

That leads me to say this. There are not only those who go that way, in the sense of organising everything and substituting human organisation for the Holy Spirit, but there are those who go to the other extreme, who use the fact that the church is an organism as an excuse for something which is loose and disorderly. This nearly always leads to indiscipline, disorder, weakness, and license. The church is not a free-for-all.

The Difference between an Organism and an Organisation

Now having said that we are presented with a mystery. What do we mean by organism? What is the difference between an organism and an organisation? "An organism is a whole," to quote the Oxford dictionary, "with interdependent parts sharing a common life." It has got an organisation, sometimes a complex and highly developed organisation, but all of its organisation develops from the life within it. All of it is formed and developed by and according to the life within.

My body is an organism. I have a most amazing organisation in this body. I have an inbuilt thermostatic control. It is the most amazing thing. If it goes haywire I would know it. If yours went haywire you would know it. It is an amazing thing. If you have ever suffered from a thermostatic control in your body going out, you start to perspire for no apparent reason and then feel cold. There is a person in this company who suffers badly from it.

You have many other things in your body that have to do with your circulation, and other functions of your body; it is a highly intricate, complex organisation. Where did it all come from? Did it read a medical book? Was it instructed in its early days by mother or father as to how it should organise itself? No, it had a life, and the whole thing within it is in the life.

Every one of you, some years ago, was just that size, a little blob of flesh and blood, but the organisation was all there; every bit of it. Every bit of you, though it's been changed every seven years, came out of that little blob, and the organisation came from within it. The only time we have to worry and read books and get ourselves diagnosed and help is when it goes wrong.

That is precisely why you have some things in the New Testament—I and II Timothy, Titus, Corinthians—because something went wrong. We have to have a diagnosis, and people have taken the diagnosis when it goes wrong as the pattern of the New Testament. It is incredible! Some people say this is the pattern that they got from the New Testament. Others say *they* have it from the New Testament. Someone else has it from the New Testament.

What is the difference between an organism and an organisation? An organisation, as we commonly understand the term, is that which is framed, set up or put together by man according to a set pattern or blueprint or a set standard of rules and regulations. Its organisation depends entirely on man. It is not from a life within but from a law applied from without. It is therefore static and dead.

A Body Compared with a Car

Now a good example is to compare your body with a car. My body is an organism, and just over thirty years ago my body was born and everything I have, except these clothes, came out of that little blob. The whole thing has come from that life. Tonight, in 1968 I have a 1968 body. You may not like it but it is a 1968 body. You have a 1968 body. You do not have a body dated the age of your birth. You have a 1968 body. It is contemporary. But if you had a car from thirty years ago it would be precisely a 1938 car in 1968 because it is an organisation; it is static. It does not renew itself from a life within. It has no way of developing or adjusting from within. It cannot do it. So it remains a static organisation in 1968. You have 1968 traffic conditions, 1968 speed, and 1968 roads in some countries, but you have a 1938 car. However, your body is a 1968 version. And if you live and the Lord tarries, in 1988 you will have a 1988 version. It will not be a 1968 one in 1988 because your body is an organism.

The church is an organism. When you look at church history, it is really like a car graveyard. All around us are various organised denominations whose organisations were built in the sixteenth century, seventeenth century, eighteenth century, early nineteenth century, and there they all are. They are all trying to go into 1968. Some of them use seventeenth century costumes trying to reach twentieth century people. They use seventeenth century language to try and reach twentieth century people, but God said, "I AM that I AM" not "I have been that I have been." He is ever present. He is the living

God, not the past God. He wants to express Himself all the time in a living, vital way.

Is There a New Testament Pattern?

Even a superficial reading of the New Testament reveals that the church is an organism, the living, functioning, growing body of Christ. The Holy Spirit is initiating, leading, filling, qualifying, gifting, empowering, anointing, developing, instructing, correcting all the way through. You will note the remarkable absence and lack of any rules or regulations in the New Testament for the setting up of a church. Now this might shock some people because they seem to think: "Oh, there must be a New Testament pattern." My friend, there is not. The only way you can get a New Testament pattern is by going through the whole thing and taking a little bit from here and a little bit from there and gleaning, and then putting it all together. Every church is built on the so-called New Testament pattern—Presbyterian, Methodist, a lot of them all built on the so-called pattern in the New Testament one way or another.

Now seeing the awful chaos which has resulted, surely somewhere in the twenty-seven books of the New Testament one small letter could have been devoted entirely to the organisation of the church. Don't you think so? Do you think God is so stupid? He could foresee all the chaos that would result. If the church were an organisation, don't you think He could have clearly said, "Now, this is the organisation of the church. This is this, that is that, and the other the other." Nowhere do we find it.

Corinthians is dealing with an appalling state of affairs, and the letter to the Corinthians would never have been written if something had not gone wrong in the church. Where did the people get the organisation to start with? In the book of Acts? Where did they get it? It developed from within. There was only one time they cast lots and that was when they filled the place of Judas. Many theologians believe that was a ghastly mistake, and ever after that we never find them casting lots again. They have the risen Head by the Holy Spirit, and they inquire of Him; He does it.

Spiritual Character and Spiritual Measure

Why were I and II Timothy and Titus written? Things had gone wrong. The apostle Paul says in the letter, "He foresees a turning away, a falling away." So he says, "Now Timothy," (he does not give regulations) "these are the qualifications—spiritual character and spiritual measure you must look for." You can be quite sure if the Holy Spirit is raising up men to be elders or deacons or for any other function, these are the qualities you will find in them. But the science or the technique of it is not there. He says, "Lay hands on no man suddenly." In other words, give time for organic development.

There is no intended blueprint in the New Testament. The New Testament does reveal principles that are inherent within the life of God. If those principles are lifted out of the life and made dead regulations and rules, the whole thing dies. But if they are kept as principles and obeyed as principles of life, then there is increase, multiplication, development, and growth.

The Onion and the Daffodil

Now I want to illustrate this with two little bulbs. I wonder how many of you would really know the difference between these two if we were to put them on a plate? You would know afterwards if you ate them, but one is an onion and the other is a daffodil. It is quite extraordinary that a daffodil has never become an onion even though they are so alike. In the whole of history a daffodil has never become an onion and an onion has never become a daffodil. Isn't that strange? You could plant a hundred onions all around this daffodil and it would still come up as one daffodil in the midst of an onion patch. You could put that one onion in the ground and plant hundreds of daffodils around it and the onion would still be an onion. Now why? Because that onion has onion life and that daffodil has daffodil life. The pattern is in the life; therefore, the pattern of the daffodil is in the life of that daffodil. When you put it in the ground, that life begins to take over and it develops always as a daffodil, and the same with an onion.

If I held a few pits in my hand, whether a pear pit, an apple pit or a few other pits, they are all so small and so alike. However when I plant them, one becomes a plum tree, one becomes an apple tree, and one becomes a pear tree. Why didn't they have a mix-up? Because there is within one of them apple life, the other pear life, and the other plum life.

The Pattern in the Life

Christ in you is the Christian life and Christ in us is the church. The pattern is in the life. Once we let the life of God start to flow through us the pattern manifests itself. You will get church life, church order, church gifts and ministries, and church increase. It will all be there; but it is the life. You do not have to bother too much about the other; it is really being together. In other words, we have to make sure we are holding fast the Head and we are allowing the life to flow through us together by the cross through the Spirit. That is why in so many of these peculiar little groups you never have church life but an awful lot of talk about it. Somewhere, somehow, some people have got to pay the price. Some have got to lay down their lives completely through the cross of our Lord Jesus and then the life starts to flow. With the life there will be building, and the pattern, and the ministry, and everything else.

Shall we ask the Lord to give us enlightenment?

Lord, we pray together that Thou wilt really give us enlightenment. We need it, Lord. Oh, that we might really understand what it means that the church is a heavenly thing. Lord, wilt Thou reveal that to our hearts and wilt Thou so work in us that we could be truly heavenly people. Again we do bring this matter of the organic nature of Thy church to You that Thou wilt really reveal this. Thou knowest that this lies at the root of so much that is broken down or failing even among so many of Thy children who long to see something of the recovery of Thy church. Oh Lord, we pray that Thou wouldst really enlighten the eyes of our hearts that we might know this thing inwardly. We ask it in the name of our Lord Jesus Christ. Amen.

4.
Organism Versus Organisation

1 Corinthians 1:9 (RV)

God is faithful, through whom
ye were called into the fellowship
of his Son Jesus Christ our Lord.
(In my estimation that is
the motto for the whole of
this letter.)

1 Corinthians 1:9 (NEB)

It is God himself who called you
to share in the life of His Son
Jesus Christ our Lord and God
keeps faith.

1 Corinthians 1:9 (Moffatt)

Faithful is the God who called
you to participate in His Son
Jesus Christ our Lord.

1 Corinthians 10:16–17a

The cup of blessing which we
bless, is it not a communion
of the blood of Christ?
The bread which we break,
is it not a communion of the
body of Christ? Seeing that we,
who are many, are one bread,
one body.
(Now that word communion
is exactly the same word
as fellowship.)

II Corinthians 13:14

*The grace of the Lord Jesus
Christ, and the love of God,
and the communion of the Holy
Spirit, be with you all.*
(The communion or the
fellowship of the Holy Spirit
be with you all.)

Psalm 122:3 (Hebrew text)

*Jerusalem that art builded as a
city that is compact together.*

Psalm 122:3

The Septuagint Version
which is the oldest translation
of the Old Testament into
Greek says: *"Jerusalem is
built as a city whose fellowship
is complete."*

I Corinthians 1:2

*Unto the church of God which is
at Corinth, even them that are
sanctified in Christ Jesus,
called to be saints, with all that
call upon the name of our Lord*

*Jesus Christ in every place, their
Lord and ours.*

I Corinthians 1:10

*Now I beseech you, brethren,
through the name of our Lord
Jesus Christ, that ye all speak
the same thing, and that there be
no divisions among you.*
(the fellowship of Christ)

Romans 12:4–6a

*For even as we have many
members in one body, and
all the members have not the
same office: so we, who are
many, are one body in Christ,
and severally members one
of another. And having gifts
differing according to the grace
that was given to us, whether
prophecy, let us prophesy.*

I Corinthians 12:12–15

*For as the body is one, and
hath many members, and all
the members of the body, being*

many, are one body; so also is
Christ. For in one Spirit were
we all baptized into one body,
whether Jews or Greeks,
whether bond or free; and were
all made to drink of one Spirit.
For the body is not one member,
but many.

I Peter 2:5, 9

Ye also, as living stones,
are built up a spiritual house,
to be a holy priesthood, to
offer up spiritual sacrifices,
acceptable to God through Jesus
Christ…But ye are an elect race,
a royal priesthood,
a holy nation, a people for God's
own possession.

Revelation 1:6

And he made us to be a
kingdom, to be priests unto his
God and Father; to him be the
glory and the dominion for ever
and ever.

Revelation 5:10

And madest them to be unto our
God a kingdom and priests;
and they reign upon the earth.

I Peter 4:9–11

Using hospitality one to
another without murmuring:
according as each hath received
a gift, ministering it among
yourselves, as good stewards
of the manifold grace of God;
if any man speaketh, speaking
as it were oracles of God; if any
man ministereth, ministering
as of the strength which God
supplieth: that in all things God
may be glorified through Jesus
Christ, whose is the glory and
the dominion for ever and ever.
Amen.

I Corinthians 14:26–33

What is it then, brethren?
When ye come together, each one
hath a psalm, hath a teaching,
hath a revelation, hath a tongue,

hath an interpretation.
Let all things be done unto
edifying [building up].
If any man speaketh in a
tongue, let it be by two, or at
the most three, and that in turn;
and let one interpret:
but if there be no interpreter,
let him keep silence in the
church; and let him speak to
himself, and to God.
And let the prophets speak by
two or three, and let the others
discern [or judge]. But if a
revelation be made to another
sitting by, let the first keep
silence. For ye all can prophesy
one by one, that all may learn,
and all may be exhorted; and

the spirits of the prophets are
subject to the prophets; for God
is not a God of confusion,
but of peace.

Matthew 23:8–12
But be not ye called Rabbi: for
one is your teacher, and all ye
are brethren. And call not man
your father on the earth: for one
is your Father, even he who is
in heaven. Neither be ye called
masters: for one is your master,
even the Christ. But he that is
greatest among you shall be
your servant. And whosoever
shall exalt himself shall be
humbled: and whosoever shall
humble himself shall be exalted.

We have been dealing with this matter of the church, His body, as an organism and not an organisation. There is a difference between an organism and an organisation. An organism is something which has an organisation. Sometimes its organisation is extremely and exceedingly complex and intricate, but all of its organisation has developed from the life within it. It never read a book; it was never taught how to go or the way it should go. Its whole organisation developed from within. An organism has got to be something living, whereas an organisation is something which is by its very nature static. It is put together from without by man or some other agency according to a blueprint or a set standard of rules and regulations or some plan. It can never change unless it is changed from without to within.

The Physical Body as an Organism

My body is an organism. Quite a few years ago it was just a little blob of flesh and blood, and now it has developed into what it is. Where did I get the whole organisation that is within my body—the built in thermostatic control, the means by which I expel foreign agencies, and all the functions of my body? Where did the organisation come from? I never read a book; it all developed from something within. If I had a car from the 1930s, today that car would be precisely a 1930's car in the 1960s. It could not change. It still has the organisation of the 1930s because it was put together according to a blueprint, a plan by men. Now that is the difference between an organisation and an organism. Some people get the idea that because we say the church is organic there should be no organisation at all. That is not correct. There is an organisation, but it is produced by the risen life of Christ and it is the Holy Spirit that makes that life of Christ real in us by the working of the cross.

Holding Fast the Head

If we would know the organic life and development of the church, we must first hold fast to the Head and then know the life of the risen Head by the Spirit flowing through at least two of us. For the church to come into being there must be at least two members. If you get two believers together holding fast the one Head and allowing the life to flow through them, before long that life will do everything. The pattern is within the life. Now the organic nature of the church covers every single aspect of its life and function. It covers, for instance, the order in the pattern.

Why have we got so many conflicting church patterns? Why do they all claim to be New Testament patterns or at least built on some system, some blueprint that has been discovered in the Word of God? In my estimation there is no intended blueprint in the New Testament. It is an extraordinary fact that in the twenty-seven books in the New Testament not one is given solely to defining the organisation, which some people would have us believe is so vital and so important. I would have thought that God, who has foreseen all the mess and chaos and confusion that has resulted, would have, in all His wisdom, devoted one of the little letters in the twenty-seven books of the New Testament wholly to defining this organisation so that once and for all we could be absolutely clear as to the church's organisation. But there is no such thing.

Order and Pattern from the Life Within

The order and the pattern—and there is an order and a pattern in the church—come through the life within. As that life progresses, develops, and increases under the headship of the Lord Jesus Christ, so the form, the order, and the pattern develop. It cannot all be set up at once.

Just think for a moment. God says, "If you have two people, saved by His grace, in Christ, holding fast to the Head on the ground of a locality, you have the church. Supposing there are only two of us Christians in Richmond. How on earth could we have elders and deacons unless I was an elder and he was a deacon? Then we would not have a congregation. Yet God says we are the church in Richmond because the two of us are members of Christ, and "where two or three are gathered together, there am I in the midst." It is the same authority, the same power, and the same life that is present where there are two or five hundred; it is precisely the same. Those two can act, if they are not ignorant, in the name of the Lord Jesus just as well as a large company.

How are you going to have all your deacons and elders and all the rest of it if there are only two of you? Do you not see how stultifying it is if as soon as you grow to twelve you decide to have elders and deacons and all the pattern? No, the pattern has got to develop from within; it cannot be set up all at once. This is the mistake so many Christians make. We have organisationalism in the blood. It is an extraordinary thing; we just cannot help it. Get two or three people together and before you know it they have to organise the whole thing according to their ideas of what the Scripture says. As soon as they do that, it stultifies and paralyzes the real flowing of the life of God. Now the thing we need to bother about is holding fast the Head. Let us keep our relationship with the Head absolutely clear and thus also our relationship with one another. Let us go on with the real job of serving the Lord together, of being built together and being used to bring others into a saving knowledge of God, then all the order and the entire pattern will take shape.

The Daffodil and the Onion

Remember, I showed you two things previously, not two onions or two daffodils, but one daffodil and one onion. These two bulbs look so alike. Why is it that no daffodil has ever become an onion and no onion has ever become a daffodil in the whole of history? How is it that these two things that look so alike and at times have been mistaken with dire results, have a different internal pattern? If we took that little daffodil and put hundreds and hundreds of onions all around it, don't you think the proximity of those onions would turn this daffodil, which looks so much like an onion, into an onion? But no; all the hundreds of onions grow up as onions and that one tiny daffodil in the middle of all those onions grows into a daffodil. If you put the onion in the centre with hundreds and hundreds of daffodils all around it, the proximity of all those hundreds and hundreds of daffodils would do nothing to the one onion; it still becomes an onion. The daffodils remain daffodils. Why is that? Because inside that dry, ugly looking thing there is onion life, and inside the life is an onion pattern and order. Inside of that daffodil bulb there is daffodil life, and inside that life there is daffodil order and pattern. These bulbs do not bother their heads about the process; they bother about living.

When brothers and sisters bother about living, they become the church. The church just flows through and the order and pattern is inside. But if instead we get our heads sort of mixed up and confused about this and that, before you know where you are, there's division and argument and everything else. Everyone is at sixes and sevens on this simple matter of order and pattern.

The thing develops and that to me is the book of Acts. Wherever you look in the book of Acts, there are differences. There was a difference between the church at Jerusalem and the church at Antioch, but it is the same basic pattern and the same basic order that spread all over the world. It did not have a little book; it was inside.

The Organic Principle

It is the same with government, the matter of elders or anything else. What happens? People say, "Oh, you must have elders." Is it not an interesting fact that we note that the apostle Paul only appointed elders on his return journey nine months after the believers had just come together and been left alone with the Holy Spirit? When he went back, he appointed elders in every city. When he wrote to Titus he said, "I have left you in Crete to appoint elders in every city." Why didn't they do it at the start? The point was that they were allowing for the organic principle. There is no greater mistake than making men elders too quickly, because once you have made a man an elder you cannot "de-elderise" him. And in many, many companies it is upon this one point that they have been shipwrecked. They have rushed ahead and made this man an elder and that man an elder. A bit later they find out it was all a terrible mistake, and the whole fellowship falls apart because of it. It is a mistake.

The book of Proverbs says, "A man's gift maketh room for him" (Proverbs 18:16a). If a man is an elder everyone knows it. In the end it filters through to everyone. It is not that everyone puts their heads together and says, "What do you think?" It is just that they know; there is something in the man. Now do not think that every elder should be like an apostle Paul. They are just ordinary people such as yourselves; but we turn to them because there is something about them that we cannot help but notice. Someone once said, "Take them apart and you would end with them all on the scrap heap, but put them together and there is something there." Government comes from the life of God within. Isn't that so? I will tell you from our own experience that we learned this.

What about ministries and gifts? They also come the same way. The gifts and ministries are within the risen life of Christ, and they are manifested by the Holy Spirit. Sometimes it has to be a breaking of the sound barrier spiritually, and suddenly the gift is manifested. It did not just suddenly drop into them. It was there in the life of Christ within them.

Let me use a natural illustration. I could give you years of piano lessons, if I were a musician, but if you do not have a gift inside, what have I done? I have just turned out a very wooden pianist because the gift is not in them. No one would ever bother to listen to them because it is wooden. But if there is a gift inside, does it suddenly drop into them when they are eight or twelve years of age? Or was it there within their temperament, within their very personality and life, and it just surfaced? Something just brought it out from within them. It is the same thing with the gift of painting, or organising ability, or any other ability or gift. It is inside a person and as they grow up it is discovered. Sometimes it is very strange as it says: "Necessity is the mother of invention." How often that happens and you are forced to do something. You cannot pay for it, but suddenly you find you have a gift. Now that is on a natural level.

The gifts are not like apples tied on a tree. God does not tie this on you or that on you. It is something that He draws out from His life within you and manifests. That is why so often the manifestation of spiritual gifts comes with the Holy Spirit coming upon a person because until now the life has been cramped and limited. Suddenly when there is a release, out comes the gift. It was there, and now it is manifested. For the church, there are all kinds of ministries and gifts. They are all locked up in the life of Christ. It is the release of His life within that we need. Get the life released by the Spirit of God, and all the ministries and gifts are manifested.

Increase Comes as the Life Grows

Then again, I must say, progress, increase and multiplication all come as the life of God grows and develops unhindered in His people. Isn't that the thing that brings men and women in? They sense the presence of God. They sense the life of God. They would not put it like that, but that is what it is. "There is something there," they say, "that I have not met before. There is something in people. It is not just preaching. It is in the people." It is the life of God.

When we first came together fully in 1953, we were more or less out from everything. We, of course, naturally believed in the New Testament pattern. So we had a week of prayer. We looked into the Scriptures and saw that they (the early church) had the Lord's table every Sunday, or at least we thought they did. It seemed to be clear that some companies in the New Testament had it every first day of the week. So we said, "We will have that." Then we said, "It is quite clear they have elders and deacons, so we must have elders and deacons." (We numbered about thirty at that time.) So we had a week of prayer and the result was that we put aside three men as elders and four men as deacons. We did it in the most spiritual way possible. We did it with prayer, a whole week of prayer and one or two of us even abstained from food. It was the most spiritual way that we could do it, and we had a perfect church pattern. Even people who knew a lot about church patterns told me that it was a perfect church pattern. As far as we were concerned, and those of you who were there in those days will bear witness to this, we were absolutely one—very, very happy, no trouble, no cloud on the horizon.

About two years after this appointment of elders and deacons, a number of us became aware of what we could only describe as a kind of spiritual earth tremor. It was something deep down within the company that seemed to be shaking us, and we could not understand it. We had such a sense that something was wrong, and yet we could not put a finger on it. In the end, if I remember rightly, one Friday thirteen of us brothers spent the day in prayer and fasting. It so happened while we were there that it began to dawn on one or two of us, as we sought the Lord, that it was something to do with this matter of the pattern, the matter of government. Yet the more I thought about it, what more could we do? We had spent a week in prayer. Surely the Lord does not expect us to spend more than that, and I had gone without some food too! After all, can you go very much further? I thought it was the most spiritual thing, the most spiritual technique possible. It was *par excellence*; was there anything better?

In the study there was a little acorn jar and in it was an acorn. It was rather like one of those hyacinth jars in which you put a hyacinth bulb in water. It was only a little thing on the study table. While we were praying, I looked across the room and saw that little acorn, and in a flash the whole thing came home to me. It was as if the Lord said to me: "Now Lance, this is the secret of the whole thing. That acorn has two kinds of unity. It has two kinds of pattern. One is the outward unity, the outward pattern which is the shell. It is static. It is incapable of producing another acorn. It is perfect, but it is static. It has all the look of the right thing, but it is static.

Inside the shell is another kind of pattern which is in the life, and if you will only let that life evolve, it will smash the outside shell and it will lose all its form altogether, but it will grow into a tree capable of producing thousands and thousands of acorns. It was the beginning of our understanding of the organic principle.

Now do not make any mistake on this. We had always taught, as some of you can bear witness who were there in the beginning, that the church is organic. But like everyone in evangelical circles, we taught one thing and practised another. The fact was that we had organised the church in the most perfectly spiritual way possible, but if you do not observe the principle, no amount of spirituality will make up for it. You can be perfectly sincere but going in the wrong direction. If you want to go to Glasgow and you are on the road to Bristol, you are going in the wrong direction even though you are perfectly sincere. It is no good someone saying to you: "Oh, how insincere!" You are perfectly sincere. It has nothing to do with your sincerity, nor is it anything to do with the quality of your character. Your character may be perfect. Nor does it have anything to do with your driving. Your driving may be absolutely marvellous, super, but you are driving in the wrong direction. That is exactly what happens, if we do not see this matter of the organic. The church is an organism not an organisation.

After that day of prayer the Lord said to us: "Now that you have seen it do not do anything; just leave it to Me." What happened? He got rid of the whole thing. In two months the whole thing went overboard, and we reverted to just being brothers and sisters. Then the most extraordinary thing happened. The one person, not a soul in the whole company would have ever thought had anything of an elder in him, suddenly began to grow head and shoulders above all the rest. It was quite extraordinary that when the one thing dissolved, the other grew. So it has gone on from that day.

Travail

Now out of that comes two things. To take the ground of the body of Christ means that we are committed to that which is organic. If we take the ground of the body of Christ, that is to say, if we are committed to that which is organic, that is, to the Spirit of life Himself, then we must understand that it is an extremely costly way, and that is why so few companies walk it. I say that because a principle of the organic is travail. Now this is precisely what the apostle Paul said. He did not shout about it from the rooftops because not everyone could understand it, but he himself knew what travail was. His co-workers knew what travail was and there were people inside those assemblies, those churches who knew what it was to travail with Christ.

Galatians 4:19 says, "My little children, of whom I am again in travail until Christ be formed in you." What a wonderful thought! "Christ be formed in you." Mark the word "again"; so he had already been in travail over them when they came into being. Now he is concerned about these churches in Galatia and he says, "I am in travail again that Christ be fully formed in you." That is travail. An organism has to be born, isn't that so? You can collect a whole lot of Christians together and say, "Here we are together; we are the church." Correct! But it is not correct in another way. Unless there are those who can travail, the organic thing can never be born in the midst. It has to be born. Once it is born nothing on earth can overcome it. That is the wonderful picture we get of the man-child born of the woman and the devil ready to devour it; then the Lord catches him up to heaven. It is a picture. I know it has another application, but the abiding principle holds stedfast that that which is born of God is invincible. "Whatsoever is born of God overcomes the world" (see I John 5:4a). That is why so few companies who start out to see the Lord recover the church in their midst go through; it is because the thing is never born. It is a costly business.

Every one of the assemblies in India came into being through nights and nights and nights of prayer. Brother Bakht Singh himself told me that sometimes people would come straight from work, get on their knees together with hundreds of others and wait before the Lord the whole night, and then go from there to work. It was forty days and forty nights of prayer before Madras came into being, and from Madras the work spread over the whole of India. The reason this matter of the church being an organism is not understood because people are not prepared to pay the price. They want much more entertainment, and they want things cheaply. They just want to be given it all, and to have everything spoon fed to them.

In Colossians 1:24 it says, "Now I rejoice in my sufferings for your sake, and fill up on my part that which is lacking of the afflictions of Christ in my flesh for his body's sake, which is the church."

Isn't that an extraordinary verse? I have often heard people refer to it as a mysterious verse: "filling up that which is lacking of the afflictions of Christ." Does it not have something to do with travail? —"for His body's sake."

Again in Philippians 3:10 Paul says, "That I may know him, and the power of his resurrection, and the fellowship of his sufferings." The word "fellowship" is *koinonia*, sharing, that I might share His sufferings. It is not, of course, His sufferings for our redemption, but it is the travail of our Lord.

I want you to note that travail is not only a principle initially, but progressively. Every single new progressive step taken in a company, a church, has behind it some kind of travail if it is going to go through the fire. Otherwise, the enemy will just come and blow on it, and it will be destroyed. It is travail which brings the lasting value into every real move of God.

Now many of you are young. You cannot travail when you are just born of God because travail is something to do with spiritual maturity. But let me say this: God has to get men and women in this company, as in any other company which He is going to use in His recovery moves in these last days, who know what it is to travail. That does not mean you go around shouting about it or wear it on your sleeve so everyone can say, "Oh, poor so and so, how marvellous it is that they suffer so much for us." You have your reward if you go around like that. It is as the Lord said, if you fast so you can be seen, you have your reward; they have seen you. It is precisely what you wanted. You wanted everyone to say, "Dear so and so, how they suffer." You have your reward; that is what you wanted. You will not get any other.

Resurrection Life

Now linked to this principle of travail is another, and it is the principle of resurrection life, the power of His resurrection. As we have said, everything is within the life of Christ and that life is His risen life. It is a life which has come through death and is on the other side of the grave. In other words, we know that life and everything that is within that life through His death. But we also know it through our death with Him, and until there are people that are willing to lay down their lives, fall into the ground and die, there can be no corporate experience of life. God is very jealous over this principle of resurrection life. In other words, every time He gets something, every time He gains some ground in someone's life, He says to the enemy, as it were, "Come on, you can do your worst; let it go back into death. Let it all come into heaviness, foulness, difficulty." There are people who would love to escape from that. They come to me and say, "What is wrong? It is all so difficult." But it is a principle of the organic.

Have you ever seen a tree that was sawn in two? Have you ever seen all the rings in it? Every ring denotes growth and the growth has been through seasons—a fresh winter, a fresh spring and a fresh summer. So it is with the organic. If you have something static you can have it pegged. There is an artificial level of joy, joy, joy, and providing you have one or two personalities that can peg it there forever, you will have it there forever. The fact is you can have that but it does not mean anything as far as God is concerned because what God is interested in is essential, genuine spiritual growth, and that comes through the organic. Therefore, we find that with the organic every time there is a growth, there is a contraction, and then a growth and a contraction. But each contraction is never less than the growth so that all the time it is solid growth. That is what we call the principle of resurrection. If you look into church history you will find again and again that every time God gets something, every time there is a move of God, He lets it go into death that the devil may prove that there is something absolutely invincible in the life of God.

In Colossians 2, Colossians 3:1–4 and Ephesians 2:5–6, 10, 14–16, 20–21, you will find the principle of resurrection. If you look at the context you will see the corporate. In the beginning it is you who are dead, you He made alive, and He raised you and made you sit together with Christ in heavenly places." He talks about "walking in works afore prepared;" then He goes on to "make of two one new man," then "you are being built upon the foundation of the apostles and prophets, Jesus Christ himself being the chief corner stone." Then He talks about "all the buildings being built together into a habitation of God in the Spirit." In other words, it is the church, and it is all to do with this matter of resurrection life.

There will be times when corporately everything comes into death, a kind of spiritual winter time, so that in that time there may be a pruning, a purifying and a purging work in order for a fresh bursting forth of divine life and power in resurrection. I think there is something so wonderful about resurrection. In the history of this company again and again we have come to a place where we thought it was impossible, finished, over; this really is the end, and yet it is amazing what the Lord has done. It is divine life. We would say, "God is unto us, the God of deliverances, and unto Jehovah the Lord belongeth escape from death" (Psalm 68:20).

Taking the Ground of the Body of Christ

The next principle we will take up is: What does it mean when we talk about "taking the ground of the body of Christ"? We mean that the church, which is His body, is the fellowship of Christ. The word "fellowship" is often, I think, grossly misunderstood, and even where it is understood it is understood only in part. I do not think it is given its full depth of meaning.

Fellowship

Fellowship is not just acquaintanceship. Some people have got the idea that fellowship is just acquaintance; we know one another.

But it is not mere acquaintanceship. It is not *bon ami*, a sort of "we are all friends; we all love each other here."

Fellowship is not talk or chatter. Some people have that idea. They say: "Let's have a little bit of fellowship." We often hear in Christian circles, "Let's have a little bit of fellowship." What it means is a cup of tea and chatter. That may be fellowship, but fellowship is not merely that, as if fellowship is just having a little chitchat and a little gossip sometimes on a higher level than that.

Nor is fellowship informality. Some people think that as soon as anyone says something about having a time of fellowship that means it is informal. Another idea about fellowship is meetings. I have often heard in certain circles when they talk about having fellowship with you it means you trot along to one of the meetings and you have fellowship. In other circles when they say, "Would you have fellowship with us?" it means would you give a word, would you preach, would you have fellowship with us?

Fellowship is not even spiritual talk. Some people think that if they can get someone sitting on the sofa and really get into the book of Leviticus, that is fellowship. But fellowship is not even only that. In fact, that might not be fellowship at all; it is a question of whether there is life in it and behind it.

Nor is fellowship a society. We often speak of *the* fellowship. There is no such thing in Scripture as *the* fellowship. It is always a description; it is not used in that way. It is quite incorrect to refer to this company as *The Fellowship*. If you look outside carved in stone you will see that "*The*" is not there; it is just Christian Fellowship. It is a description not a title.

Sharing Together

The word *koinonia* means basically "a having in common" and is variously translated in the New Testament. It means essentially "sharing;" you share. Fellowship is sharing something in common. You have something you share together. That is fellowship. It is "mutuality." It means "partnership." It means "participation in" together. It is sometimes used in this way: contribution. In other ways we think of the word just as fellowship. It is not a superficial matter to do with externals, something that is, as it were, non-essentials; and that is fellowship.

I have had people say to me: "I am not one for fellowship." I have heard ministers say that. By our very salvation fellowship should be inherently within our constitution, and when someone says, "I am not one for fellowship," they look upon it as nonessential. "Oh, let me hear the preaching of the Word and I will be there. If there is a prayer meeting I will be there; but I am not one for fellowship." In other words, "I am an individualist, and I find it very hard to really share or be linked together in a team of any kind."

Fellowship speaks of something absolutely fundamental and essential out of which all the rest comes. All those other things are in some ways fellowship in the more shallow levels. But at the root of it, in the ocean bed, as it were, there is something absolutely fundamental and essential in real fellowship out of which all the rest flows and is produced. We have been called by God into the fellowship of His Son Jesus Christ our Lord. We have been called into a participation in Him. You have been called into a participation in Him. I have been called into a participation in Him. All of us who have been saved have been called into a participation in Him.

A Participant in Christ

1 Corinthians 1:9 is glorious. What does it mean to be a participant in Christ? It means you are a member of Him; you are part of Him. You have become a partaker of His nature. You have become a partaker of His life. You have been joined to His head—one life, one body. You are now sharing Christ; that is the church. I have Christ; you have Christ; we share Him. I do not have my own Christ. You do not have your own Christ; we have only one Christ. We share the one Christ. There is no such thing as a personal Saviour. It is a foreign word to the New Testament. A personal knowledge of our one Saviour is a different matter, but there is no such thing as a personal Saviour. We all have one Lord, one Saviour, one Head, one life. We are participants in Him. I, you, all have the fellowship of His Son. Oh, if we could only get hold of this, it is so wonderful.

We have a common salvation, a common head, a common life, and a common unity. That is what we have. God is faithful through whom ye were called into the fellowship of His Son. Now it is this basic, essential, fundamental sharing of one Saviour, one Head, one life, one body which produces all the other kind of sharing. You cannot share your home with all the believers. You cannot share your car, your money, your time, or yourself with the believers unless first you recognise the essential bedrock out of which it all comes. Otherwise it is titillating, a lot of nice chatter, and then we fall out: "I am not going to talk to her again;" that kind of thing.

But when we have a common Lord and a common Saviour you cannot say "good-bye" to one another. Sometimes, it is rather sad; but that is the fact of the matter. We have to get through and that is the glory of it. The church is not the United Nations. The church is a Saviour; it has one Lord and one life, the one body.

Acts 2:44 says, "And all that believed were together, and had all things common." That is the word, *koinonia*; if you like, fellowship.

Acts 4:32: "And the multitude of them that believed were of one heart and soul: and not one of them said aught of the things which he possessed was his own; but they had all things common."

It grew out of this tremendous sense of their one Lord and their one Saviour, one life that had come to them by the Spirit of God on the day of Pentecost. They were no longer a congregation made up of units. They were a body of interdependent, interrelated parts. So they had all things in common. In this case they sold everything and more or less pooled it altogether; but the principle is the same. You are to look upon everything you have got as being the steward of it. That is why sometimes the Lord will not come in on some people's homes, and so on. They say, "Why is it? I have asked the Lord to help me in this or that." The fact is, you want the Lord as a charm, to put it rather crudely, almost blasphemously. You want Him to all the time clear up the debt. You want to have your own home, your own possessions, and what you let Him have you will let Him have. But when you are in trouble, you want the Lord there instantly to clean it all up and get it all sorted out. You say, "I am a Christian; I deserve it. Why doesn't it happen? It happens to those others; it doesn't happen to me." But the Lord will not (and this is a matter that relates to health sometimes amongst Christians), because it is a question of whether you are your own or His. Once you are His you can leave it with Him. "Lord, I am Yours, my body, my time, my money, my home; it is yours. You do something with it; it is Yours anyway. It is your responsibility." Then the Lord does.

It could well be said that I Corinthians 1:9 is the motto for I Corinthians—the fellowship of Christ. It has been called an act and comprehensive description of the church. I think it is best defined in I Corinthians 12 in terms of the body. My body is a fellowship. Every single one of the large number of members I have in my own personal body is a participant in the life and body of Lance Lambert. All these members have one head, one life, and one body. They are not yours; they are mine. You have your own. Yours are the participants in your name and life and body. It is a fellowship. Now my body is not a finger, it is not a foot and it is not an ear, but it is made up of all different parts, visible and invisible, outward and inward. But they are all there. They are all interrelated and interdependent parts sharing one life, one entity. They are a body.

God is Faithful

It says in I Corinthians 1:9: "God is faithful." What a wonderful word at the beginning of the Corinthian letter. God is faithful through whom ye were called into the fellowship of His Son, into participation in His Son, into being part of Him, being sharers in His life, in His headship, and in His body. It is written over the whole of this book with all its dark undertones, its unhappy factions and divisions.

Here we have it in this term, the body. Now a body is not one member but many, all sharing one head and one life, one entity. There is great diversity and variety of function and position. My ear has a different position than my little toe. It would be an extraordinary mistake if my little toe was in the position of my ear. There is a difference of position and function. Yet every single part of my body is interdependent and interrelated so that if I cut my hand off I can still live, but I am that much restricted. If I cut my leg off I can live, but I am that much restricted. I can cut both my legs off and I will live but I am that much more restricted. I can cut both my arms off and live, but I am that much more restricted. If I cut my head off, I am finished.

Now it is rather extraordinary. I think the devil starts by trying to cut the head off in the church, but when he cannot do that, he starts on all the members to see if he can cut them off and so bring about a paralysis in the body. It is a fellowship of that person. My body is a fellowship; your body is a fellowship. So it is with the church.

Romans 12:4–5: "For even as we have many members in one body, and all the members have not the same office: so we who are many, are one body in Christ, and severally members one of another."

1 Corinthians 12:12, 14, 20, 27: "For as the body is one, and hath many members, and all the members of the body, being many, are one body; so also is Christ ... For the body is not one member, but many ... But now they are many members, but one body ... Now ye are the body of Christ, and severally members thereof."

One Body—Many Members

The church is a body not a member. That is why when we talk about taking the ground of the body of Christ we immediately mean members. The body is many members yet one body. It is not a member but many members, yet one body. The church was never meant to be a one-man band or a one-man show as if all were meant to revolve around and centre in one member for the rest. But isn't that exactly what we see in the majority of churches, of all descriptions? Everything, virtually, surrounds one man. In the service he leads, prays, gives out the hymns. He does not always give out the notices; he generally leaves that to someone else nor does he take up the collection, but he does everything else. I have been in some groups where he has either played the piano or the organ as well. It is one member, a one-man show. Now I am not saying that people do that maliciously; of course not. But the church is not meant to revolve around one member; it is many members.

Nor was the church meant to be an elite few doing everything and the rest remain as spectators. They watch everything, listen to everything and then say, "He was good this morning. I did like the way so and so gave out the notices." It is in the hands of just a few; a few members for the rest. Everyone else is a spectator, with a kind of pulpit-pew relationship. You should be there on time, and you all just sit there; everything is done for you and to you. Then you go off like a lot of good sheep. I cannot help feeling sometimes when we view so many so-called churches, re-echoing the words of the apostle Paul in 1 Corinthians 12:19, changing the tense: "And if they [are] all one member, where [is] the body?"

Because that is exactly what you have to ask: "Where is the body?" You see a lot of little drab people all sitting there. Some of them would not say boo to a ghost, yet these are the witnesses to Christ on whom the Holy Spirit is supposed to have come with power. It is extraordinary. Now do not blame the poor folk in the pews; they have been emasculated, which is a terrible thing. They have been put into such a position that the very life has been drained out of them. The church has become one member and not many. It is a tragedy and no one can tell me that is what the New Testament teaches.

All right, you argue with me. You say you do not accept what I have said. Very well, but do you accept the finality of the Word of God? How do you explain 1 Corinthians 12? How do you explain Romans 12? How do you explain 1 Peter 4? How do you explain 1 Corinthians 14? We were never meant merely to be so many spectators for whom everything is done, rather like entertainment. We are spoon-fed. It is a tragedy in so many places, not so much in this country, but no one even brings a Bible! It is a most extraordinary state of affairs. But then I am told you cannot blame the sheep. I have been told by many theological students that you start with a verse and depart from it thereafter and never come back to it again. Do you expect people to bring Bibles if the Bible is not going to be explained or interpreted or expounded?

Priesthood of All Believers

There is absolutely no Scriptural warrant whatsoever in the New Testament for the distinction made between clergy and laity, a kind of priesthood of the few amongst the rest. On the contrary, the New Testament is quite explicit in declaring the priesthood of all believers. Now most evangelicals give lip service to the priesthood of all believers, but many of them restrict it to personal access to God in prayer, for which we are thankful that at least they give us that liberty. But the Scriptures never did mean by the priesthood of all believers that it was just and only personal access to God, glorious as that is.

What is the priesthood of all believers? It is this. Every single child of God born of the Spirit of God, every single member of the body of the Lord Jesus is a priest with the right of continual access into the presence of God Himself in the holiest place of all by the blood of Jesus. Not only that but with a continual right to serve the Lord. Now you have that in 1 Peter 2:5: "Ye also, as living stones, are built up a spiritual house, to be a holy priesthood, to offer up spiritual sacrifices, acceptable to God through Jesus Christ."

Romans 12:1–2: "I beseech you therefore, brethren, by the mercies of God, to present your bodies a living sacrifice, [a priesthood] holy, acceptable to God, which is your spiritually intelligent worship. And be not conformed to this world: but be ye transformed by the renewing of your mind, that ye may prove what is the good and acceptable and perfect will of God." It goes on to say, "For as the body has many members, yet it is one body." You have the whole matter of the body if you look at it and you will find then that you are told: Let him that does this wait on his ministry, and him that does that on his ministry. It is priesthood. Every one of you is constituted a priest. God has made us a kingdom and priests unto God by the loosing of our sins in His precious blood. Every single one of us has the right not only to come into the presence of God but to serve Him. It is the fellowship of Christ.

Shall we pray:

Dear Lord, we do ask together that Thou wilt really by Thy Spirit reveal these things to us. Make us a people, Lord, who do not just take them because they have been said, but rather those who search the Scriptures as to whether these things are so. By Thy Spirit reveal what is truth to our hearts in these days of confusion and disorder and impoverishment. Oh Father, wilt Thou make us those who understand what Thou art really seeking to do not only just the outward aspect of it, but the inward things that lie at the root of it all, those principles, Lord, in that life of Thine which must be observed if we are to know the development, growth and increase of it. Lord, we commit ourselves to Thee. In the name of our Lord Jesus Christ. Amen.

5.
The Church—
The Fellowship
of Christ

1 Corinthians 12:12–31
(J.B. Phillips)

As the human body, which has many parts, is a unity, and those parts, despite their multiplicity, constitute one single body, so it is with the body of Christ. For we were all baptized by the one Spirit into one body, whether we were Jews, Gentiles, slaves or free men, and we have all had experience of the same Spirit.

Now the body is not one member but many. If the foot should say, "Because I am not a hand I don't belong to the body," does that alter the fact that the foot is a part of the body? Or if the ear should say, "Because I am not an eye I don't belong to the body," does that mean that the ear really is not part of the body? After all, if the body were all one eye, for example, where would be the sense of hearing? Or if it were all one ear, where would be the sense of smell? But God has arranged all the parts in the one body, according to his design. For if everything were concentrated in one part, how could there be a body at all? The fact is there are many parts, but only one body.

So that the eye cannot say to the hand, "I don't need you!" nor, again, can the head say to the feet, "I don't need you!"

On the contrary, those parts of the body which have no obvious function are the more essential to health; and to those parts of the body which seem to us to be less deserving of notice we have to allow the highest honor of function. The parts which do not look beautiful have a deeper beauty in the work they do, while the parts which look beautiful may not be at all essential to life! But God has harmonized the whole body by giving importance of function to the parts which lack apparent importance, that the body should work together as a whole with all the members in sympathetic relationship with one another. So it happens that if one member suffers all the other members suffer with it, and if one member is honored all the members share a common joy.

Now you are together the body of Christ, and individually you are members of him. And in his Church God has appointed first some to be his messengers, secondly, some to be preachers of power; thirdly teachers. After them he has appointed workers of spiritual power, men with the gift of healing, helpers, organizers and those with the gift of speaking in "tongues."

As we look at the body of Christ do we find all are his messengers, all are preachers, or all teachers? Do we find all wielders of spiritual power, all able to heal, all able to speak with tongues, or all able to interpret the tongues?

*No, we find God's distribution
of gifts is on the same principles
of harmony that He has shown
in the human body.*

*You should set your hearts
on the highest spiritual gifts,
but I shall show you what is the
highest way of all.*

We have considered the question: Why are we at Halford House? We have said that we believe the Lord is out to recover something of the nature of His church before the Lord Jesus returns. Therefore, He has led us to take what we have called the ground of the body of Christ, which means in its practice and outworking, the absolute headship of Jesus Christ in His people and over His people by the Holy Spirit. That is the first thing.

The second thing is that the church, His body, is a heavenly thing and therefore inexplicable on the natural level.

The third point is the church—His body—is an organism and not an organisation.

The fourth point, which we began to deal with, was the church, His body, the fellowship of Christ. This word *fellowship*, which is used quite a lot in the New Testament, is often not understood by Christians, and where it is understood it is often not given its full depth of meaning. It is not to do with externals. It does not mean just a little bit of spiritual chatter, just a few helpful words, a kind of informal gathering where perhaps we discuss a problem. That is often what is considered as fellowship. That is included in the word fellowship, but it is not only that. It is not to do with mere externals; it is not anything to do with something just superficial. This matter of fellowship is absolutely fundamental and essential.

Called into Participation in His Son

1 Corinthians 1:9 says, "God is faithful through whom you were called into the fellowship of His Son, Jesus Christ our Lord." The word *fellowship* comes from a root meaning "to have everything in common," and it really just means "partnership, sharing, participation in." "God is faithful through whom you were called into participation in His Son."

Now if you think about that, it could be, and surely is, the theme of the first Corinthian letter. Participation in His Son is what the twelfth chapter is all about. It is what the eleventh chapter, the fourteenth chapter, and the fifteenth chapter are all about. All those problems about immorality, lawsuits, faction, and division are settled on the basis that all of you in Corinth are participants in Jesus Christ. You are all sharing the Lord Jesus Christ. That is the fellowship into which you have been called. As we said, the figure of the body that we find in 1 Corinthians 12 is the perfect example of what this word *fellowship* means.

My body is a fellowship. I have thousands of parts in my body, some visible, many invisible, some important, some not so important, but I have thousands of parts in my body. They do not all occupy the same position; they do not all have the same function, yet every single one of them shares one head, one life and one entity. It is as simple as that. My body is a fellowship. Every one of the members, parts of my body has been called into participation in Lance Lambert. Every one of the members in your body has been called, not into participation in me, but into participation in you. That is what this fellowship of Christ is all about.

The Church is a Body, Not a Member

Let us now consider that the church is a body, not a member. The body has many members; it is not one member. It was never meant to be a one-man show or a one-man band. In many places, so-called churches are merely an appendage to the preacher. The preacher is the vital all-important member. In fact, everything is concentrated on him so we can say, "If everything is concentrated on one member, where is the body?" That is precisely what happens in so many so-called churches. The church is an appendage. It consists of a platform for a ministry or a pulpit for a proclamation of the message, and everything is dependent upon that pulpit or that platform or the person who occupies it. The church is just a kind of context, a kind of necessary surrounding for that ministry or for that office; but this is not what the New Testament says. That is not the fellowship of Christ. That is not the body; that is one member, perhaps an important member, but only one member. Where are all the other members? Nor is the church one member doing everything. Neither is it a few elite members doing everything while the rest remain a bunch of spectators, sort of gazers-on who pass judgment on how well or how badly everything is being done. That is not the church either.

There is absolutely no scriptural warrant whatsoever in the Word of God for the division or distinction made between clergy and laity in the New Testament. In the Old Testament that could be argued for, but even in the Old Testament we cannot take it too far because originally the firstborn of the Levites was taken from every family to be priests. Then the tribe of Levi was chosen instead of the firstborn, and only that whole tribe was representing the whole nation.

The Priesthood of All Believers

However, when you come to the New Testament, there is no such thing as the tribe of Levi representing the whole nation, a kind of Aaronic priesthood that represents the church before God. No, on the contrary, in the New Testament we discover that every single child of God is a priest. We believe in the priesthood of all believers. Every single born-again believer is constituted by His spiritual birth a priest unto God. This is just putting the term *body* into another term, another figure. We are all priests. Every single one of us has not only the right of access to God at all times, of communion with God at all times, and of touching the throne of God at all times, but every single one of us who is born of God has the right to serve the Lord. Indeed, I would say more than that; we have the duty and the responsibility to serve the Lord. We are priests unto God.

In 1 Peter 2:5 and 9, it says, "Ye also, as living stones, are built up a spiritual house, to be a holy priesthood, to offer up spiritual sacrifices, acceptable to God through Jesus Christ...But ye are an elect race, a royal priesthood, a holy nation, a people for God's own possession."

This is the verse upon which the priesthood of all believers is based. I suppose it is true that in some form or another all the reformed churches accept the priesthood of all believers. However, it is what we mean by the priesthood of all believers where there is so much difference. The majority, while they say they believe in the priesthood of all believers, still only relegate it (and I do not like to use that word for it is tremendous) but they relegate it to having access to God. In other words, every believer has the right of access to God at all times. However, not only has every single believer the right of access to God, but they have the right to lead God's children in worship and praise and prayer. They have the right to contribute in the service of God. They have a duty and a responsibility to build up the body of Christ, the church of God.

Revelation 1:6 says, "He made us to be a kingdom, to be priests unto his God and Father; to him be the glory and the dominion for ever and ever."

"Made us to be a kingdom." We are all in the kingdom, are we not? Or is it only ministers and pastors who are in the kingdom? Are they the only ones who have been made the kingdom? Of course not! We all accept that every one of us is born into the kingdom of God; we are in the kingdom by the grace of God. Therefore, we are all priests as well.

Revelation 5:10 "And madest them to be unto our God a kingdom and priests; and they reign upon the earth." It is not just something in the future.

In Matthew 23:8–12 we have a commentary upon the priesthood of all believers, one which tends to be rather an embarrassment to many in Christian circles. "But be not ye called Rabbi: for one is your teacher, and all ye are brethren. And call no man your father on the earth: for one is your Father, even he who is in heaven. Neither be ye called masters: for one is your master, even the Christ. But he that is greatest among you shall be your servant. And whosoever shall exalt himself shall be humbled; and whosoever shall humble himself shall be exalted."

When you think of the practice amongst us Christians, and in Christendom generally, including evangelicals, we cannot say that this command of our Lord is in fact adhered to. We not only have reverends, but the right reverends, and the very reverends, and very much else which we will not go into. I understand that amongst evangelicals we do not go up as far as to say "his holiness," but all the rest we have. We also have collars turned back to front, which are very much in fashion once more. All of which means we distinguish people. We seek to give them a distinctive mark, we seem to make a difference between them and the rest of the members. I am told by many who do not agree with a priestly dress and everything else, that the reason they wear this kind of thing is because it helps them to get into hospitals. If that is the only reason for wearing a collar around the other way, what happens to people like me, poor little saints like myself and others? We get into hospitals just as easily. I am told that people in the street, these bad boys always feel it is easier to talk to someone who has a clerical collar on. Well, I wish they would talk to the bad boys and find out if that is really true! The fact of the matter is that you could make every excuse in the world, but the Word of God is absolutely plain that there is no ground at all in the New Testament for making a distinction between clergy and laity. On the contrary, as I have said, the Scripture is quite clear, dogmatically and emphatically stating the priesthood of all believers.

The Priestly Service of Each Member

Now let me say this: there is no shadow of doubt at all that there are anointed ministries and functions, gifts to the church as are stated in Ephesians 4:11, "And he gave some to be apostles; and some, prophets; and some, evangelists; and some, pastors and teachers."

1 Corinthians 12:28a: "And God hath set some in the church, first apostles, secondly prophets, thirdly teachers."

There is absolutely no shadow of doubt at all that within the church of God there are anointed ministries. Yet it is just as clear that these do not in any way detract from the priesthood of all believers. Not at all! There can be the greatest apostle but that does not for one single moment detract from the priesthood of all believers. Every single one has an equal right to go into the presence of God and the same right to serve God. Don't let us think for one single moment that an apostle has a greater right to serve the Lord than the least of God's children. We are all priests.

In Romans 12:1 we find a very interesting light thrown on this subject, which I do not think is often realised. We have here sacrificial ministry, but it is really priestly service. "I beseech you therefore, brethren, by the mercies of God, to present your bodies a living sacrifice, holy, acceptable to God, which *is* your [*spiritually, intelligent worship*]."

It was the priest who conducted spiritually, intelligent worship in the tabernacle. He was the one who received the living sacrifices. Here, you are yourself a sacrifice since you are the priest, and out of this priestly service comes the church.

A Measure of Faith

Listen to what the apostle Paul said in Romans 12:3 "For I say, through the grace that was given me, to every man that is among you, not to think of himself more highly than he ought to think; but to think as to think soberly, according as God hath dealt to each man a measure of faith." It is to each man; not one is left out.

A Gift in the Body of Christ

Romans 12:4–8 says "For even as we have many members in one body, and all the members have not the same office: so we who are many, are one body in Christ, and severally members one of another. And having gifts differing according to the grace that was given to us, whether prophecy, let us prophesy according to the proportion of our faith; or ministry, let us give ourselves to our ministry: or he that teacheth, to his teaching: or he that exhorted, to his exhorting: he that giveth, let him do it with liberality: he that ruleth, with diligence; he that showeth mercy with cheerfulness."

It seems interesting to me that out of this priestly service at the very beginning everything else flows. There is the church.

Hebrews 10:19–25 says "Having therefore, brethren, boldness to enter into the holy place by the blood of Jesus," (this is priestly service) "by the way which he dedicated for us, a new and living way, through the veil, that is to say, his flesh; and having a great priest over the house of God; let us draw near with a true heart in fullness of faith, having our hearts sprinkled from an evil conscience: and having our body washed with pure water." That is the laver as you went into the tent of meeting, "Let us hold fast the confession of our hope that it waver not;

for he is faithful that promised." Here is the body, "and let us consider one another to provoke unto love and good works; not forsaking our own assembling together, as the custom of some is, but exhorting one another; and so much the more, as ye see the day drawing nigh."

A Responsibility for the Body

The church is the body of Christ, the fellowship of Christ in which every member is a priest and has something of Christ to offer in some way and a responsibility for and toward the rest of the body, which is every other member. One day every single one of us must give account to God for the responsibility that was given to us for the church. Let not one single person in this room think that I will one day have to give account for the whole flock and for your well-being. I must give account for the ministry entrusted to me. If it is as a teacher, I ought to live in greater fear because more is required of me. The higher the office, the greater the function, the more will be required. Let no one think that one day you will stand before the Lord as a kind of spectator and watch everyone else being asked to give an account. Every single one of you is directly responsible to the Head of the body for the rest of the body. That is what we mean by the priesthood of all believers or the membership of the body. It is as simple as that.

Thus, each member shares not only the privilege and the security of a common salvation, a common life, and a common Head, but we also share its discipline and its responsibility. Discipline, because we are related to the Head and we are related to one another. The way we treat each other, the way we care for each other, the way we go through with each other is all part of that discipline for which one day we must give an answer and an account. It is not therefore one member or a few trying to do the work of the whole body; nor is it all the members trying to do one function. It is each member in his or her place functioning by the life of God within them.

A Portion of Christ

Let me put it this way. Each member has something of Christ the others do not have. Most brothers and sisters do not believe this, but it is absolutely true. Each single member, every one of us who is constituted a priest unto God, has something of Christ which the others do not have. You may not be able to see it; but just because your temperament is not the same does not mean you have nothing to contribute. Is your temperament exactly the same as someone else in the assembly? Are you precisely the same in the way you look at things, the way you feel in every way? It is a matter of temperament, of constitution, and of background. The Lord has deposited something of Christ in you, and that something of Christ comes through what you are. So, you have something to offer, something to contribute that no one else has got. You must contribute what you have of Christ for the increase and growth and fullness of the body. Now that is why one day you and I will have to give an account. It is the fullness and the growth of the body that is dependent upon the contribution of each single member. It is the multiplication, the increase in another way that is all part of this matter. It is all dependent on each one contributing what we have.

Look at I Corinthians 12:12–31, that scripture we read together in the Phillips translation, which is the best commentary on what

I am seeking to say. I am not talking about every one necessarily contributing on Sunday morning or at a prayer gathering. It is impossible, of course, and we understand that. But what we are saying is that everyone has a part to play, and even if you do not open your mouth you can be contributing something or not doing so. It is just as simple as that. Some people open their mouths when they should keep them shut. They would contribute far more if they kept their mouth shut. Others would contribute much more if they opened their mouths and let out what is in them.

The Necessity of Every Part of the Body

In the body, the ear cannot do without the eye, the foot cannot do without the hand. Every part of the body is necessary. It is not that the body cannot function without a hand, but it is that much less practical. It is not that the body cannot do without a foot, but it is that much less practical. It is false to say that the church cannot do without you. There is a sense in which it can, so let no one get big ideas; but the church will be less full. Isn't that important? You can still live without hands or feet, but you cannot do a lot. The fullness of the body has been hampered. So when sometimes there is a heaviness and dullness, do not always blame whoever is leading or speaking because so often the dullness and the heaviness is due to the paralysis in a certain number of the bodies' members. It makes for heaviness just like a body that does not have hands.

Each one has got to yield himself or herself to the others. As the apostle Paul said once of certain people in Corinth: "First you gave yourself to the Lord and then you gave yourself to us" (see II Corinthians 8:5). You have the same thing in the Word's teaching on marriage: "Giving yourself to one another." You must yield to one another. Each member must yield to the others himself or herself and all that they have of Christ, be it great or little. For the measure in which we hold back or fail to contribute what we have of Christ, allowing ourselves to be carried along by the momentum of life in the rest of the body; that is where we restrict ourselves, frustrate the Lord's purpose, and halt the building up of the body of Christ. That is a serious thing.

I do not know whether you have ever realised it before. It is just in the measure in which each member fails to contribute that there is your own limitation. So often we argue like this: If I had more of the Lord I would contribute. But the devil is so clever; he has caught you. He will snare you on that line so that you will never get a little bit more. You will just be static for the next forty or fifty years if the Lord tarries because the devil has just got you there. It is the measure in which we contribute that we ourselves grow because we belong to each other. This is the whole point. By being born into the family of God we are constituted, not only members of Christ, but of one another. So if you do not build me up and I do not build you up, I am not building myself up. I have to build you up; you have to build me up. We are to build one another up, and as we do that the body develops and grows. Don't let anyone think that they should spend their time building themselves up. That is what many think: "I have to build myself up so that I have got something." What the Lord gives you is for the others. It is not just to be put in the shop window in an exhibitionist way. May the

Lord preserve us from that kind of thing, for when you have been given something, it is for the whole body.

Sometimes what you have been given cannot be shared. Do you realise that? Sometimes there are some things that should never see daylight, yet the value of them goes through the whole body because in spirit you are not holding them for yourself. There is something that has come to you that is for the others.

The Increase of the Body

Ephesians 4:16 puts it clearly. (Be careful because we know this verse so well it sort of goes through the mind and runs off of us like water off a duck's back.) "From whom all the body fitly framed and knit together through that which every joint supplieth, according to the working in due measure of each several part, maketh the increase of the body unto the building up of itself in love."

I want first to underline one phrase: "the increase of the body," that is the operative thing. The next thing: "maketh the increase of the body unto the building up of itself." How does it make this increase of the body to its building up? "According to the working in due measure of each several part." It builds itself up; it increases according to the working in due measure of each several part—due measure, just measure, right measure. In other words, the Lord does not expect you to give any more than you have been constituted spiritually to give. Thank God for that! But woe betide you if you are not giving what the Lord has constituted you to give. That is the point. Some people run beyond themselves; other people never get there. It is "in due measure."

The Working of Each Part of the Body

Do you know the word "in due time"? The Lord was born in due time, the right time, just absolutely on the dot, in due measure. The Lord does not expect you to go beyond yourself and be extravagant. There should be a working in due measure of each several part; not just this one or that one or someone else, but in each several part according to the working. So you have a right function. It may be a small function or it may be a big function.

I believe you all know what happens when a little joint goes wrong. A little joint in my finger can just go wrong, and it is only a small thing. It might say, "Well, I am not the knee. They all despise me here; I am only a little finger, just the top joint in the little finger. I am not the knee, I am not the thigh, I am not the elbow, I am not even the wrist. I am going to quit. What happened? Of course, I am not a medical person, but a kind of arthritis sets in that top joint of the finger. It gives a lot of pain, and that little tiny joint, which refused to work, really starts to upset the body. It does not stop the whole body from working, but it does make itself felt because it is not working.

So, if you are not working you are making yourself felt. Some of you have that false modesty: "Oh, not me." You are making yourself felt more than if you worked. If you really gave what you had of the Lord we would not feel your presence, and you would flow in beautifully. Sometimes there is a spiritual psychology in this. I have a shrewd suspicion that is why a lot of people do not give what they have. They like to feel that they are at least making some kind of impression somewhere. The fact is that when the whole body is functioning, they are not conscious of all the parts of the body. It is only when they stop functioning because something is wrong with one of the parts that you become conscious of it. Isn't that so? There is a blockage; there is a stiffness; something is not flowing as it should.

It says, "According to the working in due measure of each several part maketh increase of the body unto the building up of itself." How wonderful it is when the body just builds itself up. This is what the priesthood of all believers means. This is what it means to be members of Christ and members one of another. We can build ourselves up. If the Communists came, we would have to be scattered. We could not meet here because the place would be taken away from us. However, the body should be able to build itself up. If we do not get into that way now, God help us when those days come. That is the whole point of why we feel so strongly about open times. We have to learn how to build each other up without depending upon this big brother or someone else. We are all just together. That kind of thing can go down into the catacombs; it can go down anywhere or up anywhere. The body can build itself up. But do not think that all of a sudden this will happen; stiff joints will suddenly become workable. It will not happen. You and I have got to know the Lord in experience now.

The Body is Constituted to Take and Give

In Colossians 2:19 we have the same thing: "And not holding fast the Head, from whom all the body, being supplied and knit together through the joints and bands, increaseth with the increase of God."

I want you to note, "increaseth with the increase of God." The whole body increases with the increase of God.

Then I want you to note, "being supplied through the joints and bands." The bands are the muscles, the joints are the bones, and that is how the body is supplied. It increases with the increase of God, being supplied through the joints and the bands. You are a joint or maybe you are a band. You will have to sort that one out yourself. But if something is not being supplied through you, what does that mean? You will receive something to supply it. You take something to pass it on. If my elbows or muscles would say, "we are going to be a dead sea, a dead end; we are fed up with passing things on. There is no value down on that end anyway. So, we are not going to give anymore." What happens? From my elbow downwards to the tip of my hand something starts to go wrong with that whole part. The strange thing is, nor will the elbow be happy because it has been so constituted to take, give, take, give. You as a child of God were never constituted to be a dead sea, taking all and giving nothing. You have been constituted to take, give, take, give; only get the order right. You have been so spiritually constituted that you take and give. First you must take. Do not try to give what you have not taken. When some people first become Christians, they try to give, give, give, and oh dear don't we suffer? They are giving what they have never received, and what do they end up doing? Giving themselves, and we all know it. But if first you receive, however young you are, you have something of the Lord and you can pass it on. You are a joint, a band or a muscle, and you have something to pass on to the rest.

Every part of my body is constituted on this principle that it is interdependent and interrelated. No single part lives to itself; it lives for the rest. It receives through the rest and it gives to the rest. This is the principle of the church. It is the fellowship of Christ; it is the common participation in Him. We all participate in Him. We all share Him. We all have something of Him to take and give. It is vitally necessary for the welfare of the whole body that we take and give all the time.

The Church is Called to be the Fullness of Christ

Let me put it this way. The church is called to be the fullness of Christ, and I have never failed to be amazed by this. "And gave him to be head over all things to the church, which is his body, the fullness of him that filleth all in all" (Ephesians 1:22–23).

Now this is most extraordinary. Will you note carefully that the Lord Jesus is not the fullness of the church? Now that is what you would think. It says the body is the fullness of Him who fills all in all. Now it is perfectly true that He fills all in all, but the body is His fullness. It seems almost blasphemous to say that the body of Christ, the church of God is the fullness of Him who fills all in all; yet that is what it says. If you understand the body, the church, as the fellowship of Christ, you understand the meaning.

My head finds in my body its fullness. If I had only a head I would be very cramped. I could think, I could speak and preach, but I would be very limited. Suppose my head said, "Pick up the Bible;" I could not do it. Suppose my head said, "I feel thirsty; I would like a glass of water;" I could not do it. My head finds its fullness in my hands and arms. I can pick up the glass; my head finds its fullness in my hand. My head is expressing itself in my body. Now the body is the fullness of the head. Again, if my head were to say, "I have to go outside the door," then my feet will do the job. So my head finds its fullness in the legs and the feet.

They do the job by obeying the mind of the head, and in this sense the head finds its fullness in the legs and feet. So it is true to say that the body is the fullness of its head. Your body is the fullness of your head because your body is the means of carrying out the will and the mind of your head, the means by which you express the feelings, desires and thoughts of the heart. You do it through your body.

The Expression of God's Will Through the Body

It takes the whole body, each member in fellowship with the rest, for the outworking of God's will, and purpose and the expression of His mind and thought. Isn't that challenging when you think of it? We talk so much: "Lord, let Your will be done. We want to see Your purpose fulfilled." But sometimes when we say it, the Lord says, "What can I do? They ask Me to do this, but half of them are just being carried. What can I do?" For the recovery of the church, for the rebuilding of the church, it requires that all of us, each member be in fellowship with the rest of the body joined and holding fast the Head. When that happens, the will of God is done. Isn't that true? Every time the Lord touches us in that way, things get done instantly. We are all overwhelmed and amazed. How is that so? In an instant, things that have been held up for so long just get touched. It is all just a matter of the body holding fast the Head.

In Ephesians 3:10–11 it says, "To the intent that now unto the principalities and the powers in the heavenly places might be made known through the church the manifold wisdom of God, according to the eternal purpose which he purposed in Christ Jesus our Lord."

"Through the church..." So the Lord is manifesting or expressing His manifold wisdom through the body, the fullness of Him who fills all in all. It is Christ who fills all in all. Every joint, every band, each several part is filled by Him, and as we are filled by Him we become His fullness. We become the means by which He can touch situations, He can touch a person in the office, He can touch a person in the home, He can touch a friend, He can touch the unseen powers or He can touch things on the other side of the world. He can do this; He can do that. He can do the other because the whole body is working as He orders it. It is the fellowship of Christ.

Each Member Finds Its Fullness in the Rest

I think it is the marvellous grace of God to call us unworthy sinners His fullness. Incredible! But it is even more than that. Each member finds its fullness in the others. This is something that we find very hard to swallow, but it is absolutely true. It is Christ who fills all in all. However, so wonderfully does He fill us that not one of us can be spiritually self-sufficient, but needs Him in each other. Now this is the line along which the devil always presses people, and if I may say so, it is nearly always the people who have the most. The devil pushes and presses to get them uncovered. Along what line? To make them become spiritually self-sufficient. It is as simple as that.

There are tragedies in the history of the recovery of the church in all its phases along this very line. It is because we have to learn this simple lesson that even the greatest apostle has not got everything; he has everything in the body. We have become so used to teaching Christ is my all, which is absolutely right, that we tend to think we can be spiritually self-sufficient. But you cannot. From this line of thinking grows the idea (we would never mention it) that "I am infallible. The Lord spoke and I know I am right." These people are always proved wrong. I have seen it. These infallible ones are proved wrong again and again. It is simply because we cannot accept the verdict of the church. We have the idea that somehow the Lord speaks to me and then it is fact. The rest must accept it, the rest must adjust to it because I have it.

Paul's Experience

One of the most interesting queries in the New Testament is whether the apostle Paul should ever have gone up to Jerusalem (see Acts 21). We could spend the whole time talking about this. Should he have gone up to Jerusalem? The apostle Paul was a great apostle; perhaps it would not be unfair to say the greatest. Do you know what he did? He shaved his head. What is the apostle Paul doing shaving his head? He shaved his head, took a vow and went off to keep Passover in the temple. The apostle Paul, the man who told us that the temple was fulfilled and finished with, takes a Nazarite vow, an Old Testament vow, and goes off to Jerusalem. In one place the church wept in his presence and pled with him: "Don't go up." But the apostle Paul said, "I was minded to go up." I do not know whether Luke, who was very loyal to Paul, just inserted that word "minded" in a very kind but firm way. He was minded to go up, and up he went.

In another place in a meeting of the church a prophet came up and bound Paul's hands with his girdle and said: "So this waits for you if you go up." The apostle Paul replied, "I care not what awaits me. I will go up," and he went up. He took Timothy into the temple, and there was a terrible riot. Then the apostle Paul realised a life-long ambition—he got a free ticket to Rome. It was not quite the way he expected to visit the saints in Rome or minister to them, but that is how he got there. I know that is a query; it is speculation. Some people would say that it is absolutely wrong to suggest that this was not the will of God. It is an interesting sideline, but more than an interesting sideline, it is the danger of great ministries and great anointing.

When we cannot accept the rest of the body, God help all of us in this matter. It is absolutely important for every single one of us to find fullness in the whole. I do not have everything, but I find what I lack in the others. You do not have everything; therefore, you find what you lack in the others. The Lord has so ungifted us that even the greatest ministries are still in some way dependent on others.

Diversities in the Body of Christ

1 Corinthians 12:4–7: "Now there are diversities of gifts, but the same Spirit. And there are diversities of ministrations, and the same Lord. And there are diversities of workings, but the same

God, who worketh all things in all. But to each one is given the manifestation of the Spirit to profit withal."

Not everyone is given the same thing it goes on to say. Oh, if only we were open and ready for the Holy Spirit to manifest Himself just like that: this one, that one as He will, not just and only in these things, but in every way. It is to profit with all. In other words, one finds the fullness in each other, another one finds his fullness in others. He doesn't have it all in himself.

That is why in 1 Corinthians 14:27–31 the apostle Paul tries to say, "If one of you speaks, let it be in turn." He says also about prophets, "If one has something else, let the first be quiet." In other words, do not let anyone think he is infallible and go on and on because he thinks he's got it, and the rest must listen. Let him stop and the next one come in; that is the body. These little practical things are so important.

It is the same thing in 1 Corinthians 14:24–25 about God tempering the body so that every part needs each other.

You have it again in Ephesians 3:18–19. Verse 18, a beautiful verse, says, "with all the saints." Have you ever noticed that? "...may be strong to apprehend with all the saints what is the breadth and length and height and depth." No one saint can do it. The only way to explore the breadth and length and height and depth of what is ours in Christ is with all the saints.

Then he goes on: "...and to know the love of Christ which passeth understanding." You cannot know it just yourself, but it is with all the saints. Think of it! One day when we are in glory and the whole lot are gathered together we will know it. There is the thief that was on the cross, Mary Magdalene, the apostle Paul and so many others down through the ages, all with a glorious story to tell of the life of Christ—how He found them, what He did for them, how He had redeemed them—"with all the saints." It would not be to the glory of God if only I had a story; if I said to everyone else, "Shut up everyone. I'm going to tell my story. I want everyone else to just listen and hear my story." No, but just think of the volume of praise from all the saints!

Then it says, "And to know the love of Christ which passeth knowledge, that ye may be filled unto all the fullness of God." How can one little person be filled unto all the fullness of God? Even all of us together will be swallowed up by the fullness of God. It is tremendous when you see it in this way.

Have you ever seen that strange little verse in Colossians 3:15? "And let the peace of Christ rule in your hearts, to the which also ye were called in one body." What is the connection between "Let the peace of Christ rule in your hearts," and "to the which also ye were called in one body and be ye thankful"? In other words, it is the peace of God in the whole. (Arbitrate is the word I like.) "Let the peace of God arbitrate in your heart to the which you were called in one body." It is a church matter; it is security. You find your security in the body. Let the peace of God rule in your hearts, going this way or that way, or not, but do not forget the body. That is your security.

The Sovereignty of the Holy Spirit

This matter of fellowship is one of the basic principles of the church. Fellowship of the true and full kind is the hallmark of the presence of the church in the practical outworking. You can always tell the presence of the church in its practical outworking by the presence or the manifestation of this true fellowship, this sense of belonging. With all the difficulties and failings and problems there is a sense of belonging, the sense of a building work.

If we have taken the ground of the body of Christ we must recognise the freedom of the Holy Spirit to use whom He will, how He will, when He will in the building up of the body. May I just say that once more? In this matter of the fellowship of Christ, if we have taken the ground of the body of Christ, we must recognise the freedom of the Holy Spirit to use whom He will, how He will, when He will in the building up of the body of Christ.

The Headship of Christ

I am sure this will raise a lot of questions. Let me qualify this by saying that this principle can be expressed in different ways, but it is absolutely essential because in the end it is a matter of the headship of Christ in His people. If the Lord wants to use this one, He must be able to. If He wants to use that one, He must be able to, when He will, how He will. But that does not mean, as some people think, that every time ought to be an open time. Let me say this very, very clearly because I think it needs to be said. I believe the Brethren made a great mistake in thinking that every gathering should be a free-for-all. The principle is this: the Holy Spirit must be sovereign in the matter of whom He uses, how He uses, when He uses. But there is such a thing as oversight. There is such a thing as the headship of Christ expressed and vested in brethren. There is such a thing as objective.

For instance, I have been in times of prayer which were on the principle of a free-for-all. We sit and wait. Someone suggests a hymn, someone suggests another hymn, then someone has a little word of praise, then someone gives a little reading. No one gives any suggestions, but suddenly someone says they have had a letter from somebody and they read it out. The time comes that you do not know where you are. Now we have to ask ourselves a question: "Is that what the Lord wants?" To me, a prayer time has got to be conducted like a military operation, but with the principle of the sovereignty of the Holy Spirit to have the one whom He wants to lead, and to lead, is right. In a prayer meeting we are all taking part. It is the objective which is the point.

Now I have seen and have been in these other meetings where there has been such a loss. I have even been in an open-air meeting conducted on this principle. It was the worst fiasco I have ever been in. It was tragic because it was a complete misunderstanding of the principle. The result is that all the saints, especially those who have life in them, are groaning about it. Why do you think so many of the Brethren pour into Baptist churches and other Free Churches to listen to good preachers? I can tell you of one place in Glasgow, Scotland where half of the evening congregation are Brethren. They all deserted their own place to go and listen to a good Church of Scotland production. How could the people who believe in the freedom of the Holy Spirit and everything else darken the door of such a place? It is because they are entirely fed up with this kind of lax, loose, dull, dreary meeting that goes on and gets nowhere. A recognition of the freedom of the Holy Spirit must not be mixed up with a free-for-all. It is the objective of a time that determines how or whether a time should be entirely open.

The Exercise and Expression of Each Member

Let me put it another way. Place must be given in the life of the church for the exercise and the expression of all the members of Christ under Christ's headship. Whether it is once a week, twice a week or three times a week, whatever it is, place must be given; in other words, where it is absolutely free and open for all to take part as they are led of the Lord. But surely the whole point is this: if there is going to be evangelism, it has to be led. If there is going to be a prayer time it must be shared—surely it must be shared. Let us be free for the Lord to use who He will, but the fact is that certain things have to be done in order that we can get down to the real substance—prayer and fulfillment of this warfare of the service. That is the point. The principle behind it is recognition of the absolute sovereignty of the Holy Spirit. That is why we should always pray for those who have responsibility in times which are not open that they really know the mind of the Lord and may be kept from making such mistakes.

As far as the open times go, you have it in 1 Corinthians 14:26–32: "What is it then, brethren? When ye come together, each one hath a psalm, hath a teaching, hath a revelation, hath a tongue, hath an interpretation. Let all things be done unto building up. If any man speaketh in a tongue, let it be by two, or at the most three, and that in turn; and let one interpret: but if there be no interpreter, let him keep silence in the church; and let him speak to himself, and to God. And let the prophets speak by two or three, and let the others discern. But if a revelation be made to another sitting by, let the first keep silence. For ye all can prophesy one by one, that all may learn, and all may be exhorted; and the spirits of the prophets are subject to the prophets."

That simply means there is no such thing as this disorderly kind of uncontrolled frenzy. "The spirits of the prophets are subject to the prophets." It is different, of course, when the Holy Spirit sometimes comes on a people like a flood as He does, as it were, almost like a bomb. That is different. Generally speaking, as it says here: in the gatherings of the church, there is order. For instance, how can a person who has a tongue keep silent if we have this idea that suddenly it bursts out of them like a bomb and they cannot help it? They know that there is no interpreter; they have to keep silent. In other words, there is a certain amount of spiritual intelligence exercised.

In 1 Thessalonians 5:19–22 it puts it like this, and it is obviously to do with an open time: "Quench not the Spirit; despise not prophesyings; prove all things; hold fast that which is good; abstain from every form of evil."

The greater ministries in Ephesians 4:11—apostles, prophets, evangelists, pastors and teachers must be given scope for their building up of the body of Christ; but the ordinary members of the body must also be given ample scope so that the body may build itself up in love.

Trusting the Holy Spirit

I think it is important for us to understand the principle that lies behind all of what we have been saying. Sometimes I think we tend to feel that when the Lord gives us something we have to keep our hands on it; otherwise it will be lost. This is distrust in the sovereignty of the Holy Spirit. Oh, how I wish sometimes that people would not give a long reading and then a long prayer. This is not the body, and it actually arrests the body. We should only follow a reading with prayer when we are convinced. It is the exception not the rule, unless it is in prayer when we are standing on a particular sentence or verse. Otherwise, give over to the body. Two or three times when someone has been reading, I have known in my spirit such a kindling has come into my heart, but it has been killed by the same person going on and on. Haven't you found that? It was killed and yet it was so of God. The person who gave that something, which was so much of God, killed it. Now how is that possible? They did not recognise the principle of fellowship, the membership of the body. This is the whole problem of infallibility again. Let go. Let go. Do you have something? Let go. See if the Holy Spirit takes it up. Do not just think that you are everything. Let go and let the Holy Spirit do it. If He does not do it, perhaps you were wrong. But you will find that if it really was of God, you will be rekindled to take up that matter. There is such a blessing once you let go in this matter.

It is a wonderful thing when the Holy Spirit sweeps in and leads a company, and you hear a portion of the Word and someone takes it up in prayer and then another and another. The other matter is like a person who speaks in a tongue and gives the interpretation. You always feel, "Well, we are a little suspicious of it. Are they trying to put something over?" But when someone speaks and someone else interprets, there is a wonderful witness; there are two witnesses. In the mouth of two it shall be established, and that is the body. So suffer that little word; it is all to do with this matter of the fellowship of Christ. We have each got something.

The Manifestation of the Holy Spirit

The Holy Spirit wants to manifest Himself in the gathering. We are all used to it. He manifests Himself in prayer. How do you pray? It is surely not just a dead sort of thing, but something comes into your heart and you feel you must pray about it. You pray and then it moves on, and someone else prays. While you are praying, if it really is alive, someone else is kindled, (forgive the word kindle, but it is the best word I think) and someone else gets kindled. Why do we do that in prayer and in nothing else? The time on Sunday morning should be just the same as this. The most glorious times we have are when someone hears from the Lord and then someone else, and then someone else and we move on. Oh, that is wonderful! The most wonderful times we have had surely are when we have found the Lord's mind. The Lord spoke to this one, and then that one, and then the other; it cannot be any clearer. We all have to learn these lessons.

Now someone may say to me: "Yes, but just wait. It is all very well to say that, but if you let go of something the Lord has really given you, it could be lost, couldn't it? It is precisely what happens in a time of prayer isn't it? You can pray something and some young one in the Lord comes in and, oh dear, the thread is lost. What needs to happen? We have to trust the Holy Spirit to come right in and bring us back. It is not the fault of that young one; they just did not understand it. They said something and we are off the rails; but come back onto the rails again. The Lord is not the least bit bothered about the young ones or anyone else when it is not malicious. Of course, when there is someone who is sort of a blockage, that is a problem to the Lord. But when it is just that we say something out of order, well, thank God for people who make mistakes. It is better to have people jumping in where angels fear to tread and we learn from it, than all sit there waiting to become spiritual and it never happens.

All Things Done unto Building Up

I think it is important that we see that there is one simple law which harmonises this great variety and diversity of gift and function in the fellowship of Christ. You have seen the tremendous difference of ministry, gift, function, position in the body of Christ. There is one simple, little law which, if it is obeyed, harmonises everything, keeps us all in the way of life and sees that the objective of it all is accomplished. It is the simple law, the standard by which we can judge every work and contribution. It is contained in 1 Corinthians 14:26: "Let all things be done unto building up." That is a simple little word, but it is the simple which harmonises everything. The thing that harmonises everything is building up. Anything that is exhibitionist is destructive. Anything that is just a person trying to put over an opinion is destructive. Everything that is someone just trying to influence people is destructive. Let all things be done unto building up. This is the standard by which we can judge everything.

Don't you think it is a wonderful thing that every single one of us is a member of His body? Some have been on the road for years, spiritually. And there are some who have only been saved a year, but they are no less members than those who have been saved for many years. They are just as much a priest. They do not have as much experience, but they are just as much priests. That is rather wonderful, isn't it? Every one of us has something to give. The Lord is not concerned with everything being done just right. He wants everything to be done decently and in order, but He is not concerned with a beautiful liturgy and everything just perfect. What He wants is a flow so that there is a working in due measure of each several part. It is not only the great ministries from one brother or another brother to the whole, but the whole family building itself up by that which every joint and band supplies. May the Lord help us.

Shall we pray:

Dear Lord, we do commit this to Thee. We do need Thy help, Lord; Thou knowest that. We do praise Thee that Thou hast made us members of Thyself and members one of another. Lord, help us in this matter. We want to be released, Lord, from all that holds us back. Thou hast said that grace has been given to each one of us according to the gift of Christ. Lord, oh that we might use that grace that is given to give, to minister what Thou hast given us of the Lord Jesus Christ in due measure. Lord, we bring our cry to Thee. Oh Father, wilt Thou release such a flow of Thy life through us all. We pray that where there is blockage Thou would give light on it to each one. If it is because we are not giving what we are receiving, Lord, help us. If there is some issue, some shadow that is holding us back and spoiling things, give us grace to come right through it. But we do pray that there may be a wonderful free way for Thyself to build up Thine own through every single one. And we ask it in the name of our Lord Jesus Christ. Amen.

6.
The Oneness of Christ

John 17:11, 21–23

And I am no more in the world,
and these are in the world,
and I come to thee. Holy Father,
keep them in thy name which
thou hast given me, that they
may be one, even as we are...
That they may all be one;
[those who believe Me through
their word] even as thou,
Father, art in me, and I in thee,
that they also may be in us: that
the world may believe that thou
didst send me. And the glory
which thou hast given me I have
given unto them; that they may
be one, even as we are one;
I in them, and thou in me,
that they may be perfected
into one; that the world may
know that thou didst send me,
and lovedst them, even as thou
lovedst me.

Ephesians 2:14–16, 18

For he is our peace, who made
both one, and brake down the
middle wall of partition,
having abolished in his flesh
the enmity, even the law of
commandments contained in
ordinances; that he might create

in himself of the two one new man, so making peace; and might reconcile them both in one body unto God through the cross, having slain the enmity thereby:...for through him we both have our access in one Spirit unto the Father.

Ephesians 4:3–6

Giving diligence to keep the unity of the Spirit in the bond of peace. There is one body, and one Spirit, even as also ye were called in one hope of your calling; one Lord, one faith, one baptism, one God and Father of all, who is over all, and through all, and in all.

Hebrews 2:11

For both he that sanctifieth and they that are sanctified are all of one: for which cause he is not ashamed to call them brethren.

Romans 12:4–5

For even as we have many members in one body, and all the members have not the same office: so we, who are many, are one body in Christ, and severally members one of another.

1 Corinthians 12:12–13

For as the body is one, and hath many members, and all the members of the body, being many, are one body; so also is Christ. For in one Spirit were we all baptized into one body, whether Jews or Greeks, whether bond or free; and were all made to drink of one Spirit.

Galatians 3:27–28

For as many of you as were baptized into Christ did put on Christ. There can be neither Jew nor Greek, there can be neither bond nor free, there can be no

male and female; for ye all are
one man in Christ Jesus.

John 15:1, 4–5

I am the true vine, and my
Father is the husbandman...
Abide in me, and I in you.
As the branch cannot bear
fruit of itself, except it abide
in the vine; so neither can ye,
except ye abide in me. I am the
vine, ye are the branches:
He that abideth in me, and I
in him, the same beareth much
fruit; for apart from me ye can
do nothing.

1 Corinthians 10:16–17

The cup of blessing which we
bless, is it not a communion
of the blood of Christ?
The [loaf] which we break,
is it not a communion of the
body of Christ? seeing that we
who are many, are one
[loaf], one body: for we all
partake of the one [loaf].

Colossians 3:10–11, 15

And have put on the new
man, that is being renewed
unto knowledge after the
image of him that created him:
where there cannot be Greek
and Jew, circumcision and
uncircumcision, barbarian,
Scythian, bondman, freeman;
but Christ is all, and in all...
And let the peace of Christ rule
[arbitrate] in your hearts,
to the which also ye were called
in one body; and be ye thankful.

Romans 15:5–7

Now the God of patience
and of comfort grant you to
be of the same mind one with
another according to Christ
Jesus: that with one accord ye
may with one mouth glorify the
God and Father of our Lord
Jesus Christ. Wherefore receive
ye one another, even as Christ
also received you, to the glory
of God.

Romans 14:1

But him that is weak in faith receive ye, yet not for decision of scruples [doubtful disputations].

Philippians 3:15–16

Let us therefore, as many as are perfect [full-grown] be thus minded: and if in anything ye are otherwise minded, this also shall God reveal unto you: only, whereunto we have attained, by that same rule let us walk.

I have entitled this lesson, "The Oneness of Christ—the Positive Exclusion of All Man-made Barriers and Divisions." Christ is the oneness of all true children of God. The Scripture is emphatically clear that the body is one because there is only one Christ and He is one. There is only one Christ and because He is one then the body is absolutely one; He is indivisible.

In 1 Corinthians 1:13 Paul asks a question. You will see that in some of the versions it has been put in different ways, but here in the Standard Version it is put like this: "Is Christ divided?" It should be literally: "Christ divided?" Impossible! Christ divided? Was Paul crucified for you? Just as Paul was not crucified for our salvation, so Christ cannot be divided.

One Body in Christ

We have the same thing in 1 Corinthians 12:12: "For as the body is one, and hath many members, and all the members of the body, being many, are one body; so also is Christ."

Again in Romans 12:5: "So we, who are many, are one body in Christ, and severally members one of another."

All the members of Christ's body share Him as their common salvation, their common Head, and their common life. He is their unity. Our oneness does not, in the final analysis, depend on our temperaments, or our backgrounds, or our nationality, or our cultural or racial background, or the way we were brought up. Our unity is not just a matter of agreeing to agree. Our unity is something far deeper than mind or reason or thought. It is in a Person and in a life—a shared Person, a shared life. We are all by the grace of God in Christ and Christ is in all of us. That is our unity; nothing less than that and essentially nothing more.

The Unity Between the Father and The Son

So essential and so profound is the nature of this unity that we are told in John 17 it is precisely the same unity as that which exists between the Father and the Son. No one can define the unity that exists between the Father and the Son and the Son and the Father. That is profound, but it is essential. The unity that is ours is exactly the same.

John 17:11b, 21a, 23a: "... that they may be one, even as we are ... that they may all be one; even as thou, Father, art in me, and I in thee, that they also may be in us ... I in them, and thou in me, that they may be perfected into one."

John 14:20: "In that day ye shall know that I am in my Father, and ye in me, and I in you."

I have often thought that this verse is one of the most wonderful verses in the Bible. "In that day ye shall know that I am in my Father, and ye are in me (in the Father,) and I (and the Father) are in you."

John 14:23: "Jesus answered and said unto him, If a man love me, he will keep my word: and my Father will love him, and we will come unto him, and make our abode with him."

Verse 17 says, "the Spirit of truth." The Spirit of truth is also given to us; therefore, we have the whole triune God—the Father in Christ by the Holy Spirit in us. That is the profound and essential nature of the unity which is ours. It is not just likened to the unity between the Father and the Son; it is precisely the same.

This Unity is Organic

It is clear therefore that this is not an organized unity, but an organic unity. We cannot create it of ourselves nor can we attain to it by our own efforts or our own ingenuity. It is already ours in Christ and He is indivisible. Our unity is not just trying to get alongside of each other or trying to be nice to each other or trying somehow to agree with each other. Basically, our unity is that Christ in you is the same Christ who is in me; it is ours. If we abide in Him we cannot be divided, but if we get out of Him we are divided.

This Unity is a Fact

This spiritual unity is a fact and not an objective. Oh, the mistake that has been made in Christendom by making unity an objective instead of seeing that it is a fact from which we move out, a fact upon which we stand. It is not just an objective to reach out toward, but it is something which has already been won for us. It is an indisputable spiritual fact to be experienced because it is Christ Himself to be known by the Spirit. We are to give diligence to keep what has already been given to us in Christ. It is as simple as that.

Give Diligence to Keep this Unity

Ephesians 4:3 says: "Giving diligence to keep the unity of the Spirit in the bond of peace." Note the word *keep*. You cannot keep something you do not have, can you? You cannot keep a nonexistent job. You cannot keep a nonexistent house. The word is "maintain," if you like. You cannot maintain a nonexistent car. If it says give diligence to keep the unity of the Spirit, the first thing you have is the unity of the Spirit, then you keep it, then you give diligence to keep it. If you are going to be very careful about the maintenance of your car, the first thing you have to have is the car; then you can maintain the car, and then you can be careful to maintain the car. "Give diligence to keep the unity of the Spirit." The unity of the Spirit is there. We may fall away from it; we may get out of Christ, but the unity of the Spirit is there; it is a spiritual fact already given to us in the Person of our Lord Jesus Christ. We can only be divided when we leave the position God has given us in Christ and come down to another level, to the earth, to the level of the carnal.

1 Corinthians 3:3: "For ye are yet carnal: for whereas there is among you jealousy and strife, are ye not carnal, and do ye not

walk after the manner of men? For when one saith, I am of Paul; and another, I am of Apollos; are ye not men?"

1 Corinthians 1:12: "Now this I mean, that each one of you saith, I am of Paul; and I of Apollos; and I of Cephas; and I of Christ."

Carnality is just flesh. If you and I get out of our position in Christ, if we do not hold fast the Head and simply come down to what we are naturally, we shall be divided within a matter of days. We can never heal division by simply trying to come together horizontally. We have to do it through Christ. When we get right with Christ, we are immediately right with one another. It is a way to judge, and the way we can judge everything is by that. People have much vaunted spirituality, but if they are out of gear with other children of God that spirituality is in a measure "pseudo spirituality." For no one can be in touch with the Head in a living way, holding fast to Him, and really be divided from other believers.

Born Into this Unity

Furthermore, let's make this point: every true child of God has been born into this oneness. John 3:3, 5: "Verily, verily, I say unto thee, Except a man be born again, he cannot see the kingdom of God...Verily, verily, I say unto thee, Except a man be born of water and the Spirit, he cannot enter into the kingdom of God."

1 Corinthians 1:30: "But of [God] are ye in Christ Jesus, who was made unto us wisdom from God, and righteousness and sanctification, and redemption."

"But of God are ye in Christ Jesus, who was made unto us." You are in Him and He is in you. You are in Him and God makes Him everything to you in this so great salvation. He is wisdom, He is righteousness, He is sanctification, He is redemption; He is all, and we are born into this oneness.

1 Corinthians 12:13: "For in one Spirit were we all baptized into one body, whether Jews or Greeks, whether bond or free; and were all made to drink of one Spirit."

You and I have been born into this unity of the Spirit. If you are a child of God, you and I have been born into this oneness of Christ. We entered it when we were born of God. There is no such thing as entering in later. We entered it when we were born of God even if we were ignorant of that fact, even if we did not recongnise the fact that we were born into this oneness. In fact, as far as God is concerned we were born into the oneness of Christ. The moment you and I, though simple, sometimes weak, sometimes very ignorant, put our trust in the Lord Jesus Christ as our Saviour and our Redeemer, that moment God put us in Him and made Him to us all these wonderful things. We are not only living in a union with Christ but in a union with one another.

Now I suppose most evangelical Christians accept the fact that having been born of God they are in a union with the Lord Jesus Christ. But the whole point is it cannot stop there, because you and I have been made one with Him, we are one with His body. Since you and I have become members of Christ, we are members one of another. Because you and I have become a branch in the vine, we find all these other branches in the vine. Because you and I are living stones we discover all the other living stones.

Romans 12:5: "So we, who are many, are one body in Christ, and severally members one of another."

Have you thought of that? Just in the same way that you are a member of Christ, you are a member one of another. I am one of your members, you are one of mine, because we are members of Christ's one body.

Who is Included in This Unity?

This union includes every true child of God, however weak or ignorant that one might be, and it excludes every single one not born of God, however knowledgeable or religious that one might be. We may get some shocks one day when we find out just who is in that oneness and who is not. Thus, let us be absolutely clear that every single true child of God whoever they are or whatever label they might have, however weak or ignorant they might be, is included in that oneness. Every single one who is not born of God, however knowledgeable, whatever position they might occupy in the ecclesiastical hierarchical system, if they are not born of God they are excluded from that oneness. Christ has never been, and never will be, the unity of believer and unbeliever. He will never ratify any division between believer and believer. Let's put that clearly.

II Corinthians 6:14–18: "Be not unequally yoked with unbelievers: for what fellowship have righteousness and iniquity? or what communion hath light with darkness? And what concord hath Christ with Belial? or what portion hath a believer with an unbeliever? And what agreement hath a temple of God with idols? For we are a temple of the living God; even as God said, I will dwell in them, and walk in them; and I will be their God, and they shall be my people. Wherefore come ye out from among them, and be ye separate, saith the Lord. And touch no unclean thing; and I will receive you, and will be to you a Father, and ye shall be to me sons and daughters, saith the Lord Almighty."

The Lord Jesus Christ is not, and never will be, and never has been, the unity of believer and unbeliever. So any kind of membership that includes unbelievers is something that God does not recongnise for one single moment. His Word is absolutely clear: "Come ye out from among them and be ye separate, saith the Lord." Nor will the Lord ratify, as I have said, any division between believer and believer, however traditional or however hoary with age or however novel, however much it is justified or excused by Christians. He absolutely and emphatically refuses to ratify any such division on any level whatsoever, anything that divides a believer from a believer or believers from believers.

The Middle Wall of Partition

Ephesians 2:14: "For he is our peace, who made both one, and brake down the middle wall of partition, having abolished in his flesh the enmity, even the law of commandments contained in ordinances; that he might create in himself of the two one new man, so making peace; and might reconcile them both in one body unto God through the cross, having slain the enmity thereby."

Christ died to break down and abolish the middle wall of partition. Now, there is a middle wall of partition in this house[1]. It divides two rooms. It is a middle wall of partition. If there was not a door in it we could not go to the other room. It is just like

1 Halford House

down the whole of this house which is divided completely from one end to the other end by a middle wall in which we are not permitted to have a door due to an antiquated law in days when chastity was common in this country before marriage. If we were to knock one single door into that wall we would lose the license to marry people. No building in this country of the British Isles is permitted to be licensed as a place where marriage can be solemnized if it has a connecting door with a residence; it is a middle wall of partition. It means that every time we want to get into that house we have to go around the garden or out into the street and walk around to the front door in that part of the house.

But the Lord died to abolish such spiritual middle walls of partition. The things that make everything difficult, the things that hinder everything, the things that stop the flowing together, the things that stop the unity of His life and headship being expressed, He died to abolish them. He died to break them down, pull them down, tear them down from the top to the foundation and abolish them. The wall of partition was not just pulled down so a new stronger one could be built up because it had become weak and rather tottery. He broke it down that He might abolish it altogether, and so make of two one. That is what He did. Now the question is this: Can we, dare we, rebuild such walls? He died to produce this living inward, organic, dynamic oneness. We are not to contradict it. We are not to destroy that oneness in any way, but rather we are to diligently maintain it.

Only Three Reasons for the Division of Believers

Geographical

Let us carefully note that in the Word of God there are only three reasons given or three grounds for the division of believers or the exclusion of believers from the gathering together or the assembling of God's people. The first is geographical. That is the only ground in the Word of God for the division of believer from believer. It is a question of where you live. We are not really divided, but we are divided in the sense of our coming together. Obviously, the people in Tokyo and the people in England cannot come together in quite the same way. We have to settle local matters here, and the folk in Tokyo or New York or somewhere else have to settle it there. That is one ground.

Disciplinary

The second ground is disciplinary. In 1 Corinthians 5:9–13 we read this: "I wrote unto you in my epistle to have no company with fornicators; not at all meaning with the fornicators of this world, or with the covetous and extortioners, or with idolaters; for then must ye needs go out of the world: but as it is, I wrote unto you not to keep company, if any man that is named a brother be a fornicator, or covetous, or an idolater, or a reviler, or a drunkard, or an extortioner; with such a one no, not to eat. For what have I to do with judging them that are without? Do not ye judge them that are within? But them that are without God judgeth. Put away the wicked man from among yourselves."

Disciplinary action is one of the grounds for the exclusion of someone who has been saved and is a child of God, but who is living in sin.

Heresy or Apostasy

The third ground in the Word of God for the exclusion of believers or division from them is heresy or apostasy.

I Timothy 1:19–20: "Holding faith and a good conscience; which some having thrust from them made shipwreck concerning the faith; of whom is Hymenaeus and Alexander; whom I delivered unto Satan, that they might be taught not to blaspheme."

Romans 16:17: "Now I beseech you, brethren, mark them that are causing the divisions and occasions of stumbling, contrary to the doctrine which ye learned: and turn away from them (e.g. withdraw from them)."

Revelation 2:2: "I know thy works, and thy toil and patience, and that thou canst not bear evil men, and didst try them that call themselves apostles, and they are not, and didst find them false."

II John 9–11: "Whosoever goeth onward and abideth not (notice that) in the teaching of Christ, hath not God: he that abideth in the teaching, the same hath both the Father and the Son. If anyone cometh unto you, and bringeth not this teaching, receive him not into your house, and give him no greeting: for he that giveth him greeting partaketh in his evil works."

There are only three grounds in the Word of God for the division of believers or the exclusion of believers—geographical, disciplinary, heresy or apostasy. Apart from those three grounds there is no other ground for division or exclusion of a single child of God. Anything more than this, which excludes true children of

God from gathering together, is wrong; anything which includes those who are not true children of God is wrong.

This Unity is Practical, Realistic, and Dynamic

This oneness of Christ, this unity which Christ has produced in Himself, is not a vague, unrealistic, abstract, idealistic thing. So often, especially if you have been brought up in evangelistic circles, you get the idea that this unity is something invisible or intangible and therefore it is abstract, it is something up there. No one ever really sees it but it is there; you sort of take it by faith. This is not so. This oneness which Christ has produced in Himself is practical, realistic and positively dynamic. Once the unity of Christ finds a way of expressing itself, it is absolutely dynamic. It dynamites everything. It blasts away right through all that would divide us, whatever it is, whatever realm it is.

We are not to relegate this matter of unity to the future: one day when the Lord Jesus comes, then this perfect unity that exists between the Father and the Son and us is going to be manifested. Nor are we merely to relegate it to the unseen and the intangible, but it is to be experienced, expressed, and maintained in concrete ways in time and on this earth. It is just here that the devil has done his most devastating work amongst us Christians, dividing us and dividing us and dividing us. It seems to me that the devil hates the unity of Christ, as if he knows that if he can fragment Christ he can paralyze things, hold things up, make things difficult whether locally or universally, whatever it is, whatever sphere it is. You and I have to understand that all the earthly and natural barriers which divide man from man have been swept away in Christ.

The New Man is Corporate

Colossians 3:10–11: "And have put on the new man, that is being renewed unto knowledge after the image of him that created him: where there cannot be Greek and Jew, circumcision and uncircumcision, barbarian, Scythian, bondman, freeman; but Christ is all, and in all."

Take note of these wonderful words. This new man is not a personal man; he is a corporate man. It is the church; it is Christ, Head and body. We put Him on, and as we put Him on we discover that in Him are all the other members. We are suddenly in a body; we are suddenly in a family—a spiritual family, an eternal family. But more than that listen to this: "where there cannot be Greek or Jew, circumcision or uncircumcision, bondman, freeman, but Christ is all and in all."

I will just run through a number of different versions on this verse.

Authorized Version:
Where there is neither Greek nor Jew, circumcision or uncircumcision, barbarian, Scythian, bond or free.

American Standard Version:
Where there cannot be.

The Twentieth Century New Testament:
*In that new life there is no distinction between
Greek and Jew, circumcised, uncircumcised,
barbarian, Scythian, slave or freeman.*

Weymouth:
In that new creation there can be neither Jew nor Greek.

Moffatt:
*In it there is no room for Jew and Greek,
circumcision and uncircumcision.*

Williams:
*In this new creation there is no Greek or Jew,
circumcision or uncircumcision.*

Phillips:
*In this new man of God's design there is no
distinction between Greek and Hebrew, Jew or
Gentile, foreigner or savage, slave or freeman.*

The New American Standard Bible:
*... a renewal in which there is no distinction
between Greek and Jew.*

Goodspeed:
*Here what matters is not "Greek" and "Jew," the
circumcised and the uncircumcised but Christ.*

Then, this is how "Christ is all and in all" is put:

Moffatt:
Christ is everything and everywhere.

Goodspeed:
Christ is everything and in us all.

Monsignor Knox:
There is nothing but Christ in any of us.

Phillips:
Christ is all that matters for Christ lives in them all.

Twentieth Century New Testament:
But Christ is all! And in all!

Natural Barriers Are Abolished in Christ

All those natural barriers that divide man from man have been abolished in Christ. They cannot exist. They have been done away. The middle walls are gone.

Galatians 3:28: "There can be neither Jew nor Greek, there can be neither bond nor free, there can be no male and female; for ye all are one man in Christ Jesus."

Ephesians 2:15b: "... that he might create in himself of the two one new man." Create in himself of the two one new man.

Racial Barriers

What are these barriers essentially that divide man from man? We have racial barriers—white, black, Asian, African, European, American—that tend to divide us in one way or another. They are very, very deep-seated. People talk about all the troubles and so on, but when it starts to hit them they feel very differently. Everyone can offer good advice until the real problem comes. But it is not just a matter of cleanliness or anything like that. It is often a matter of cultural background—the way we do things, the way our minds think, the clash of two cultures, the clash of two ways of living. They are deeply rooted within our very being.

National Barriers

There are national barriers. We all play down national barriers today. The younger a nation is the more patriotic it is on the whole. This is not a day so much of nationalism, but you know it is still there. We just put a foot wrong with someone about their country, and they can be very upset and very annoyed because national temperament, national traits, national character are very deep-seated things. There is animosity between nationalities.

Social and Religious Barriers

There are social barriers such as class, sects, and all the rest of it. There are religious barriers, not only of Buddhist, Confucian, or Muslim, but denominational barriers—Baptist, Congregationalist, Roman Catholic, Anglo Catholic, Lutheran, Wesleyan, Brethren— all these different things. These are all barriers that divide us. So, we either look down or we look up.

Personal Barriers

There are personal barriers that are between us. There is no such thing as African Christians in God's sight; there are only Christians in Africa. There is no such thing as Asian Christians, only Christians in Asia. There is no such thing as European Christians; there are only Christians in Europe. There is no such thing as British Christians; only Christians in Britain. There is no such thing as Danish Christians, only Christians in Denmark. There is no such thing as Japanese Christians, only Christians in Japan. It is a way of looking at it. Once we say Japanese Christians, British Christians, German Christians, French Christians, we are all divided. We are simply Christians, are we not? We know it when the true family of God meets together. It does not matter what nationality or race or social class is represented, we are one. What a wonderful thing it is when everyone is mixed up together, titled or untitled; all just jammed together. Everyone has something to give and no one is standing on what they are. I have known that and many of you have, and it is very wonderful. Of course, we set up religious barriers, but when they are gone, and from our different backgrounds we each have something to give, to contribute, it is Christ who is everything and in everyone.

Personal barriers are where all our troubles come from in the end because those are the deepest seated of all; they are deeply rooted in our constitution and temperament. Even when the Lord has dealt with race, nationality, social class, sects and religious denominations, there are still those things within us that hit up against the others. However, Christ in Himself, by His work on the cross has abolished every barrier and division and made us one in Himself. How has He made us one new man? He has done it in Himself. In other words, we are in Him and He is in us and that is our unity.

Division is a Sin

Let me put it again like this: He is our unity. Therefore it follows that division on any level is not just sad evidence of failings to be lamented and borne with patience. Division is not just something wrong but unavoidable to be accepted. It is sin! It is sin! That is why I could not be a Baptist another day. I am not saying for others, but for myself. In the day that I saw that to have a label was dividing Christ, that day the label went. I would rather go into the presence of God as a despised, nameless Christian than to have any number of the labels that are going round amongst Christians and to be guilty of being any part at all to the dividing of Christ.

There is this common idea amongst us that these divisions are hoary with age, part of human nature and you cannot do anything about them. However, you know as well as I do that in every age, in every generation in the history of the church, there has been an expression of universal unity. Sometimes they are the most despised people, persecuted, and martyred, but amongst those who have been simple, ordinary, honest, godly people, there has been that expression of the oneness of Christ. It is there that the lampstand has been all the way through church history.

I can only say that it is a building again of that middle wall of partition. It is not only the building again of such middle walls of partition, (I'm talking about division, being in it or part of it) it is the acceptance of them or the adjustment to them. Those things simply mean if you are building again that wall or any part of it, if you and I are accepting it as something to be lamented over but cannot be helped, or adjusting ourselves to it, then we are undoing the work of Jesus Christ. That is why it is sin. To go out and get drunk means that you have sinned against your body; but to divide Christ is to sin against His body, and therein lies the solemn and serious nature of this whole matter. Such an acceptance of division, however it may be excused or justified by some, divides Christ, hinders and frustrates God's purpose, halts the building of God's church, denies Christ's full and finished work in its practical outworking and consequences, and stumbles the unsaved. You know as well as I do how most people say to us, "Well, if Christianity is true, why is it so divided? Why is there so little love shown between them?" Most people, the men in the street, do not distinguish between nominal Christians and true Christians, between church goers and those who really do know the Lord.

Anything denominational, sectarian or exclusive, must of necessity, due to its very character, divide believer from believer. It is not necessarily a question of malice but a question of constitution. If an idiot punches you in the eye, it is not necessarily a matter of malice; it may be a question of constitution. He is demented, so he punched you in the eye. He did not know any better. People seem to think that because we say that anything denominational or exclusive or sectarian is wrong and sinful we are being very sanctimonious. We are not saying it is necessarily malicious; it is constitutional. It is something that comes out of the very way these organisations and institutions are constituted.

Anything which makes the standard of fellowship or membership a question of a certain measure of light, of knowledge, or experience extra to the essential minimum inherent in new birth, is divisive. Nearly all that is denominational or sectarian or exclusive is built in this way. So, we get denominational church constitutions. We get denominational church creeds and declarations. We have the membership roll. We have the membership qualifications and conditions. They vary from group to group, but you have these things which are instruments of division. That is what I mean by them being constitutional. It is not that it is malicious; it is constitutional. It goes right back to whether a thing is organic or organised.

The Basis for Fellowship

The basis for fellowship together in Christ is not the unity of the faith and of the full knowledge of the Son of God. That is something that we are going to arrive at one day or attain unto. The basis for fellowship together in Christ is the unity of the Spirit into which we have been born of God.

Ephesians 4:13: "Till we all attain unto" (is the Revised Version, the American Standard Version, and all the modern versions) "the unity of the faith, and of the full knowledge of the Son of God."

Ephesians 4:3a: "Giving diligence to keep the unity of the Spirit."

The Two Unities

We have two unities. One we are told we have; therefore, we are to keep it, to maintain it. The other we are told we are arriving at; we are coming to. One is a goal; one is a basis. Now the trouble with so much of Christendom is that we have made the goal the basis, and therefore we have been divided. If we were to take this small company within these four walls and make a unity of the faith and of the full knowledge of the Son of God our basis for fellowship, I do believe we would have immediately two or three churches so-called. We could not help it. It is the unity of the Spirit into which we have been born of the Spirit of God. That is the basis upon which we fellowship together. Therefore, because of the oneness of Christ, we must receive all whom He has received. That is what it means in practice.

Receive Everyone Whom the Lord Has Received

Romans 15:7 puts it very simply in these words: "Wherefore receive ye one another, even as Christ also received you."

We, therefore, because of the oneness of Christ, because we have been born into this oneness, must receive everyone else whom the Lord has received. In other words, the one requirement we need, the one necessity for fellowship together, for being looked upon not as a visitor but as a member of the family is: Has the Lord received you? If the Lord has received you, God forbid that any of us should reject you. We can do no other. You might be very untoward, very difficult or awkward, but what can we do? We are trapped. If the Lord has received you we must. Woe betide us if we reject you. Has the Lord received you? If the Lord has received you, if you have been saved by the grace of God, if you have been born of His Spirit, if you have been received by Christ, we must receive you.

It does not matter who it is—someone that has been in the Church of Scotland, or the Archbishop of Canterbury or the Pope. We accept them all if they are received of God. If God has received them, we have received them. If God has not received them, we will not. Be absolutely clear about what I am saying. I am not talking about pushing people out. We are talking about whether a person is a member of the family. I am not talking about those difficult occasions when someone comes that we just do not want to see, but so often in the world it can be like that. But I am talking now about the normal family when someone comes as a visitor. Now often we show more politeness, more courtesy and more love to a visitor than ever we do to our own family. The kind of thing when someone comes in with a hat that you really wonder where on earth they got it from, but the whole family clucks and coos over them. However, if a member of the family came in with that hat on they would say, "Get that out of this place! You look awful. You are a member of the family." The same hat could be clucked and cooed over on a visitor, but on a member of the family you get it straight from the soul.

We do not accept as members anyone who has not been born of God. We will do everything we can by the grace and love of God to make a visitor welcome, no matter who it is. With the greatest religious dignity in the world, if they are not saved, we will welcome them as a visitor to the family; but we must receive every single one whom the Lord has received, therefore we have no membership. We cannot put our membership in the Lamb's book of life. We can only go by the fruit that we see. "By their fruit you shall know them," says the Lord. We have to go by that witness of the Spirit and the fruit that is seen in lives.

Receive One Another as Christ Received Us

Will you also note that we must receive one another as Christ received us? Now here is the key to the whole matter, and I might say sometimes the crunch. We must receive one another as Christ received us. How did Christ receive me? He received me as a sinner saved by grace. He did not receive me as someone who could preach or someone who thinks he could preach. He did not receive me as someone who perhaps thinks he is knowledgeable or someone who is zealous or someone who is devoted or someone who is going to be useful. He received me as a worthless, insignificant, ugly sinner. That is how He received me. It was the minimum basis. He received me as a sinner saved by grace. Here is the equality of fellowship. Every single one is received on the minimum. What is the minimum? The minimum is that you are a sinner saved by grace; not that you are decent, and devoted, and pure, and spiritual, but that God saved you as a sinner who could not save himself or herself.

It is a sad fact that the way the Lord has received you and me is not the way that we have received one another, and hence all our trouble. For all the time, we judge one another. We cannot receive one on that basis. But that is the basis upon which we are to receive one another, and we fellowship together in Christ. Are you a sinner saved by grace? That is the operative thing, saved by grace. Are you a sinner saved by grace? Has He received you as a sinner saved by His grace? Then we receive you in the same way on that one basis of what He is.

Receive Not for the Decision of Scruples

Romans 14:1: "But him that is weak in faith receive ye, yet not for decision of scruples."

This is exactly what happens—"for the decision of scruples." It is an investigation into their conscience. Isn't that exactly what happens with most membership conditions? I was investigated by two people, and I got in on a two-thirds majority. It was the only way I got in.

"Him that is weak in the faith" That is the very person that some of us will say, "Oh, very wobbly." We will get him in the corner and say, "Now look here. Have you given up drinking? Do you go to the cinema?" This is the kind of thing that happens, and I have known it. I have even seen a poor girl, who did not wear something on her head, taken out and grilled by two old sisters. It was not here, thank the Lord.

"Him that is weak in faith receive, yet not for decision of scruples." In other words, not for doubtful disputations, having a good old argument with them trying to convince them they should do so and so to make them more acceptable. Him who is weak receive as Christ received him as a sinner saved by grace. Let God do the work of investigating. Let God do the sorting out of the motive. Let God do all the work of reformation and cleaning up. Oh, the trouble we get into. Someone comes in with a troubled background and we say something about divorce or something else, some unhappy background, and before you know it there are people latched on to them drumming up the divorce laws. It is incredible! Him that is weak receive, yet not for doubtful disputation, not for decision over scruples.

Scruple is interesting, isn't it? You may have a scruple about smoking or drinking which may be from the Lord, but do not take someone else in for a decision over scruples. Receive him as Christ has received him or her.

Paul, who could have argued with all of us and cut the lot of us off, says in Philippians 3:15–16: "Wherefore let us therefore, as many as are perfect, be thus minded: and if in anything ye are otherwise minded, this also shall God reveal unto you." That is the spirit of the apostle Paul. If we are really moving forward we will be together in this, but if you are otherwise minded, we are not going to argue about it. We are not going to have decisions of scruples or doubtful disputation. We will leave it; the Lord will reveal it, either to you or me. We go on. "Only, whereunto we have attained, by that same rule let us walk."

So, if God has said to you: "Don't you do that," you do not do it. If God says, "You do so and so," you do it. But don't all the time be saying, "If I cannot do it, he cannot. Why should he be doing it and I can't?" So what we do is we judge him. Isn't it strange that people who take drugs always want everyone else to take them? Or they want to get them all into the same club. It is a human tendency. So if the Lord has dealt with you over something, don't try to get them all in the club of the non-whatever it is. It is a destruction of fellowship and oneness. This is where the fly is in the ointment. More trouble is here than anywhere else.

Unity Versus Uniformity

I think we should add just one little point: this unity is not uniformity. I always think that wherever there is uniformity it is an evidence that true organic unity is not there. True unity is expressed in variety and diversity in the unity. If you think about that you will see it is true. There is a tremendous variety and diversity of gift and function of operation in the oneness of Christ.

To take the ground of the body of Christ means in practice that we stand in the oneness of Christ having left all that is a contradiction to that oneness, all that could or would divide in any way on any level. It means that we receive everyone whom He has received and minister to all to whom He ministers. It means that we want to be able simply to greet and to welcome every other born again believer as a member of Christ with us and to seek to draw each one in as a member of the same body, the same family.

We see this beautifully exemplified in the book of Acts where there is a unity and great variety in diversity from beginning to end. We see it in all parts of the Word, this rebuking by the apostle of any lining up behind names or personalities or teachings as such. We see it exemplified in the breaking of bread, the Lord's table. Perhaps some of you who are younger in the Lord forget that one of the supreme testimonies of the Lord's table is one loaf and one cup. We share the bread, and we share the wine. It is one loaf and one cup, and we share it together. What are we doing? We are simply saying we have been born into this oneness. We have been born into Christ. He is ours. May the Lord help us.

Shall we pray:

Now Lord, we just simply commit ourselves to Thee and pray, beloved Lord, that Thou wilt reveal this to our heart, and do not let it remain in the realm of theory or doctrine or just Biblical knowledge. Lord, we pray that by Thy Spirit Thou wilt enlighten the eyes of our heart that we may know this inwardly. Lord, we know how important this matter of oneness is, and we ask that Thou would help every one of us to give diligence to keep the unity of Thy Spirit in the bond of peace. We ask it in Thy name. Amen.

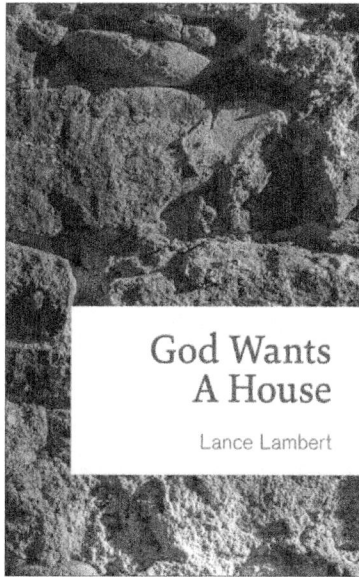

God Wants A House

Where is God at home? Is He at home in Richmond, VA? Is He at home in Washington? Is He at home in Richmond, Surrey? Is He at home in these other places? Where is God at home? There are thousands of living stones, many, many dear believers with real experience of the Lord, but where has the ark come home? Where are the staves being lengthened that God has finally come home? In *God Wants a House* Lance looks into this desire of the Lord, this desire He has to dwell with His people. What would this dwelling look like? Let's seek the Lord, that we can say with David, "One thing have I asked of Jehovah, that will I seek after: that I may dwell in the house of Jehovah all the days of my life, To behold the beauty of Jehovah, And to inquire in his temple."

Other books by Lance Lambert can be found on lancelambert.org

"If Any Man Would Follow Me ..."

Battle for Israel

Be Ye Ready: Imperatives for Being Ready for Christ

Called Unto His Eternal Glory

Evangelism

Ezra - Nehemiah - Esther

Fellowship

Gathering Together Volume 1: Christian Fellowship

Gathering Together Volume 2: Christian Testimony

God Wants a House

How the Bible Came to Be: Part 1

How the Bible Came to Be: Part 2

In the Day of Thy Power

Jacob I Have Loved

Lessons from the Life of Moses

Let the House of God Be Built: The Story and Testimony of Halford House

Living Faith

Love Divine

My House Shall Be a House of Prayer

Preparation for the Coming of the Lord

Qualities of God's Servants

Reigning with Christ

Spiritual Character

Talks with Leaders

The Battle of the Ages

The Eternal Purpose of God

The Glory of Thy People Israel

The Gospel of the Kingdom

The Importance of Covering

The Last Days and God's Priorities

The Prize

The Relevance of Biblical Prophecy

The Silent Years

The Supremacy of Jesus

The Uniqueness of Israel

The Way to the Eternal Purpose of God

They Shall Mount up with Wings

Thine Is the Power

Thou Art Mine

Through the Bible with Lance Lambert: Genesis - Deuteronomy

Till the Day Dawns

*Unity : Behold How Good and How Pleasant
- Ministries from Psalm 133*

Warring the Good Warfare

What Is God Doing?: Lessons from Church History

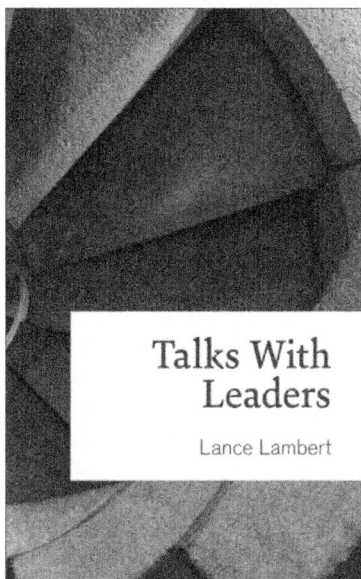

Talks With Leaders

"O Timothy, guard that which is committed unto thee …" (1 Timothy 6:20) Has God given you something? Has God deposited something in you? Is there something of Himself which He has given to you to contribute to the people of God? Guard it. Guard that vision which He has given you. Guard that understanding that He has so mercifully granted to you. Guard that experience which He has given that it does not evaporate or drain away or become a cause of pride. Guard that which the Lord has given to you by the Holy Spirit. In these heart-to-heart talks with leaders Lance Lambert covers such topics as the character of God's servants, the way to serve, the importance of anointing, and hearing God's voice. Let us consider together how to remain faithful with what has been entrusted to us.

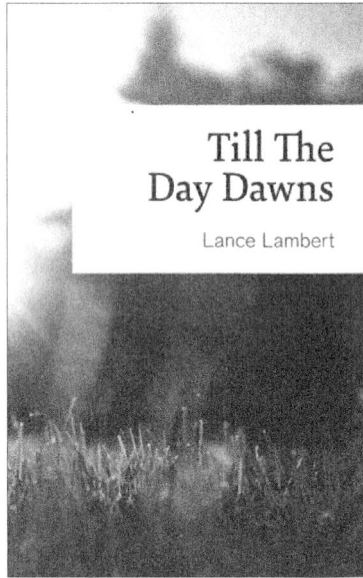

Till the Day Dawns

"And we have the word of prophecy made more sure; whereunto ye do well that ye take heed, as unto a lamp shining in a dark place, until the day dawn, and the day-star arise in your hearts." (II Peter 1:9).

The word of prophecy was not given that we might merely be comforted but that we would be prepared and made ready. Let us look into the Word of God together, searching out the prophecies, that the Day-Star arise in our hearts until the Day dawns.

Printed in Great Britain
by Amazon